WEIRD U.S. LAWS

Strange, Bizarre, Wacky & Absurd

Winter Prosapio and Lisa Wojna

BLUE
BIKE
BOOKS

The Publisher: Blue Bike Books
Website: www.bluebikebooks.com

Library and Archives Canada Cataloguing in Publication

Prosapio, Winter, 1962–
    Weird U.S. laws : strange, bizarre, wacky & absurd / Winter Prosapio and
Lisa Wojna.

ISBN 978-1-926700-40-3

    1. Law—United States—Humor. I. Wojna, Lisa, 1962–
II. Title. III. Title: Weird United States laws.

K184.P76 2012   349.73'0207   C2012-904880-1

Project Director: Nicholle Carrière
Project Editor: Kathy van Denderen
Cover Image: gavel and court room: © moodboard / Alamy;
bride and groom: © Thinkstock
Illustrations: Roger Garcia, Peter Tyler, Patrick Hénaff, Pat Bidwell, Craig
Howrie, Djordje Todorovic, Graham Johnson

Produced with the assistance of the Government of Alberta,   **Government**
Alberta Multimedia Development Fund   **of Alberta** ■

We acknowledge the financial support of the Government of Canada through
the Canada Book Fund (CBF) for our publishing activities.

                                    ■✦■   Canadian   Patrimoine
                                          Heritage   canadien

PC: 1

DEDICATION

To Adam, Sierra and Mireya,
who inspire many wacky laws in our house.

–WP

To JS. Mama loves you.

–LW

ACKNOWLEDGMENTS

A huge thanks to the amazing folks at Blue Bike Books for inviting me to be part of such a fun project, to Lisa, my partner in words, and to the most patient editor in the world, Kathy van Denderen.

–WP

To the folks at Blue Bike Books, our amazing editor, Kathy, and to a great writing partner, Winter. This great team made this project a fun escape into the past!

–LW

CONTENTS

Introduction

For a relatively young country, the elected representatives of the United States have never held back from issuing laws as they saw fit. Whether it meant outlawing metallic balloons or regulating the length of hotel sheets, lawmakers have been quite industrious when identifying situations that require legislation.

In this book you'll find laws that are outdated, oddly worded or in complete conflict with a little document called the Constitution. Some of the laws will make you laugh, others will make you cringe, but most of them, we think you'll agree, are just plain weird!

Most of the laws we found seem largely unenforced until, unexpectedly, they are—like the law about cursing that had been on the books for decades and long forgotten. Forgotten, that is, until a man fell out of his canoe and started cursing a blue streak.

Throughout book you'll note such references as "Class B misdemeanor" or "Class C misdemeanor." Misdemeanors are divided into classes, the most serious of which is Class A. Those crimes carry the highest penalty and could include jail time. If a person is convicted of a Class C misdemeanor, on the other hand, it is a relatively minor charge and may only involve a modest fine, although jail time isn't totally out of the question.

Misdemeanors are the one place in life where shooting for a C is better than landing an A! More serious crimes jump from Class A misdemeanors to felonies. Felonies generally involve prison terms. Felonies also have classes, varying slightly from state to state. Short of crimes having to do with explosives and weapons, most of the laws in this book fall into the misdemeanor category.

You'll also find places where we cite a law that we've found through numerous reliable sources but fell just short of proving its existence outright. Therefore, you should be within your rights to hunt camels in Arizona, though we do not recommend breaking any of the laws in these pages to see if they are, in fact, still in force.

★ ★ ★

Animals:
Wild and Domesticated

While the Laws of Nature follow their own sense of logic, the laws of the land feel no such restraint. For centuries, communities have tried to place some sort of limit on the occasionally awkward interactions between citizen and beast. Everything from bear wrestling to dogs smoking cigars has garnered enough attention that legislatures felt compelled to act. Some laws actually have a good (yet still funny) rationale, but others just have us wondering why in the world people would drive around with gorillas in the backseats of their cars?

THE WILD AND WOOLY

Don't Wrassle that Bear, 'Bama!

Back when the West was wilder and largely unsettled, bear wrestling was an exhibition type of event. Most people presumed bear wrestling went the way of the Wild West shows and chuck wagons. However, *Sports Illustrated*, which, after all, considers itself a bit of an expert on wrestling, notes that wrestling between man and bear has continued underground. Some amateur wrestlers apparently can't give up the allure of tangling with a bear.

Of course, most bear wrestlers don't exactly step into the ring without taking a few precautions. Stories abound of bears being declawed and having their teeth removed and their tendons severed, all of which presumably would even the odds.

Frankly, once you defang, declaw and cripple a bear, it might be more dangerous to wrestle a 300-pound bag of sugar.

Given the cruelty to the bears, the Alabama legislature in 2006 decided something needed to be done to shut down the matches. Current Alabama Code Section 13A-12-5 spells out unlawful bear exploitation as a situation when a person knowingly "promotes, engages in or is employed at a bear match." If money is exchanged for either wrestling a bear or training and selling a wrestling bear, the individual is running afoul of the law.

And it's no mere slap on the wrist. Unlawful "bear exploitation" is a Class D felony, which will make it the oddest thing to pop up on a background check. The bears are moved from the wrestling ring to the custody of a "society which is incorporated for the prevention of cruelty to animals."

I Swear, Officer, I've Only Got Five Squirrels

It's clear that Arkansas has a lot of people who love their pets. But even in the state known as a place where "People Rule," there are limitations on pet love. For example, it's against the law to own a large carnivore, such as a bear, lion or tiger.

Another limitation in the state is around the small, furry carnivores such as raccoons, gray foxes, red foxes, coyotes and bobcats. Folks in Arkansas are allowed to have up to five small carnivores— presumably of each, though the law is not quite clear on this. Also subject to the no-more-than-five rule are squirrels, rabbits, quail, possum and deer.

Fortunately for all the reptile lovers out there, alligators are not considered large carnivores nor are they subject to the five-or-less rule. It's possible the reptile lobby has a strong presence in Little Rock, the state capitol.

However, you can't keep your alligator—or alligators as the case may be—in the bathtub. So break out the kiddie pool for your alligator congregation ("congregation" is the official collective noun for a large group of alligators).

RUMORED
No Camels During Rush Hour

It seems likely that this is one of those urban legend laws, but rumor has it that it's illegal to walk your camel around Palm Canyon Drive in Palm Springs, California, during rush hour between 4:00 PM and 6:00 PM.

Are You Sure That's a Cat?

Exotic pets are popular in some parts of the country, but in Prince William County, Virginia, there's a limit. Actually, there are many limits. Every wild animal from a skunk to a tarantula is illegal to keep as pets in this county. Also on the list are monkeys, raccoons, wolves, squirrels, foxes, leopards, panthers, tigers, lions, lynx, poisonous snakes, alligators and their crocodilian brethren as well as "any other warm-blooded animal" found in the wild.

Ferrets and lab rats are among the excluded animals, as long as they've never "known the wild."

Rhino Pet Permits

Most children will beg their parents for a dog or cat. But fortunately for parents in Norco, California, they've got a perfect out if their little one pleads for a rhinoceros. Anyone who wants a rhino in Norco needs a $100 permit from the city.

Also on the "not allowed without a permit" list are hippos, elephants, ocelots, alligators and "any other animal of wild or vicious propensities."

The law was enacted in 1988. Norco residents are well known for keeping exotic animals, some of which have been known to escape their pens.

OH DEER!

Dry Land Only

Deer hunting is a big business. Ranchers lease out their land to hunters during deer season and carefully cultivate their wild herds.

There are a few limitations on deer hunting, however.

In Florida, hunters are not allowed to kill a deer while swimming. Apparently, dining on deer while swimming is an activity restricted to crocodiles. Just kidding! The law actually refers to when the *deer* is swimming.

Arkansas also prohibits killing deer when they are paddling across water. It's a bit unsportsmanlike, plus it'll be a little tough to get your deer out of the lake afterwards!

Leave the Key Deer Alone!

The adorable, miniature Virginia whitetail deer that live on the Florida Keys are so cute! And endangered. And it's a felony to molest them. These deer wandered down to the Keys during the Wisconsin Glacier period thousands of years ago, making their way across a long land bridge. When the Wisconsin Glacier melted, the deer were left on small islands we now know as the Florida Keys. Thanks to the lousy vegetation, the deer ended up shrinking over time to about 30 inches tall at the shoulder. Like many Floridians, they are great swimmers.

Most Key deer live on Big Pine Key and are so fearless that it's likely they'll be the ones doing all the molesting, always on the lookout for an obliging tourist with some carrots. And even though the deer are endangered, it's a felony to feed them even a single carrot (or anything else), set out water for them, or try to keep them from decimating your landscaping. Jimmy Buffett convinced lawmakers to lower the speed limit on Big Pine Key to reduce the number of Key deer hit on the roads.

No Deer Dragging!

If you do have the misfortune of hitting a deer while driving in Topeka, Kansas, you may want to make sure you're not on Kansas Avenue. It's illegal to drag a deer across that street.

HUNTING GUIDELINES

Aim a Little to the Left!
No, Your Other Left!

Hunting has a long, proud tradition in the U.S. The activity has become so common that there is a big effort to ensure that everyone can take part in hunting, particularly in Texas. Blind people can legally hunt in Texas, as long as they have someone with them who can see.

To Ticket or Not to Ticket?

Laws were created to make life easier. When rules are written in black and white and clearly explain what is and is not acceptable, it leaves little room for debate—at least that's the theory. Legislation about the dos and don'ts of lion hunting in South Dakota did little to answer questions that rose after a lion was killed in that state.

A story on Field & Stream's website in January 2012 told of how Shannon Secrest, a ranch hand in Harding County, killed a mountain lion he discovered up a tree on his neighbor's land. Concerned for the safety of his livestock, Secrest shot the lion after his dogs warned him of its presence. He then reported the kill to the proper authorities and, believing he'd done nothing wrong, proceeded to plan to have his trophy mounted.

Of course, nothing is ever as simple as it seems. Although Secrest had a legitimate and current lion permit issued to landowners for use on their property when they believe their livestock is being threatened, officials in this case wondered whether the cat was really a threat at all. Officials further questioned the caliber of rifle Secrest used to shoot the lion—it was a lighter caliber than what is allowed for hunting lions in South Dakota. Officials haggled over the fact that Secrest admitted that his dogs alerted him to the cat's presence; in South Dakota it's against the law to use dogs to hunt for lions.

As of the writing of this book, the jury is still out on whether Secrest can keep his cat, or if he'll get a ticket for his troubles. In either case, the moral of the story is the same: when a law is as clear as mud, you'd better sift through the fine print before taking aim at your target!

Going Up!

If you want to take a shot at a bison out of your hotel window, make sure you get to at least the third floor. It's illegal in Texarkana, Texas, to shoot a buffalo from the second story.

Fly-by Shooting?

If you think flying overhead will give you the advantage over your prey during hunting season in Nevada, think again. Shooting any "birds or animals while flying in an aircraft" has been outlawed in this state since 1973. As with most regulations, there are exceptions to the rule. The "hunting, killing or non-lethal control of coyotes, bobcats or ravens from an aircraft" is permitted, providing the proper authorities are doing the shooting.

WATERY WILDS

Get a Net!

Some laws seem as though they were written mostly to try to deal with a lack of common sense, or at least an underdeveloped sense of self-preservation. In Maine, it's illegal to catch lobsters with your bare hands.

At first grab, this seems to be a fairly odd restriction. However, according to biologists, the law has a basis in preservation. Lobster fishermen have had a strong history of working to prevent lobsters from being overfished and have petitioned for strict laws regarding their capture. The reason it's illegal to catch lobsters with bare hands is because divers can "hand pick" the best lobsters and leave the less desirable ones in the water. Soon the waters would be filled with leftover lobsters, which would produce more undesirable lobsters.

Something Fishy

There are many weird laws regarding the treatment of marine animals in the U.S. Some of them seem to be focused on unlikely, or difficult, activities.

For example, in Tennessee, it's illegal to lasso a fish. It may be that lassoing a fish is easier than it sounds; perhaps fish are not as slippery as their slimy scales would indicate. Still, it's hard to imagine there would be many ropers in the state that would be up to the challenge.

Then again, in Kentucky, you can't fish using a bow and arrow. This method of fishing is more common than most people realize. Difficult, to be sure, but still fairly common. The toughest part is knowing how to aim because of the refraction of the water. The common advice is "aim low, then aim lower." Unless one is in Kentucky, of course, where the advice is "get a hook."

Tasty—With a Kick

In Los Angeles, it's illegal to lick toads. At least the ones that secrete a hallucinogen.

I've Got a Bite! Literally!

In Texas in 2011, "noodling" came up from the muddy depths of illegality when the governor signed HB 2189, the Noodling or Handfishing Law.

Finally, after decades of being threatened with fines of $500 for catching catfish with their hands, Texans can now stick their hands into the murky water and grab one by the gills. Noodling, also known as hogging or grabbing, is legal in some form in 11 states, but the sport isn't without controversy. The concerns have to do with the method of "fishing."

Noodlers, working from either a boat or in the water, find an underwater catfish hole, stick their arm in the hole and wait for a catfish to clamp down on their hand. Noodlers then drag the catfish literally by the throat—the inside of the throat—and toss it into the boat. Catfish caught this way can be huge, nearly 50 pounds, and getting one into the boat is often a two-person job.

While anglers protested the law's passage, claiming that it's not particularly sportsmanlike given that the catfish can't escape, catching catfish with your hands is not exactly safe for noodlers either. Other marine life enjoy living in catfish holes, including animals with a bit more bite. Some of the dangerous lodgers include muskrats, snapping turtles, snakes and beavers. One noodler reported needing 13 stitches in his hand after encountering a beaver that packed slightly more dental work than a catfish.

Thar She Blows!

Some states don't let a little detail such as lacking a nearby ocean deter them from enacting laws to protect marine life. In Oklahoma, whaling has been illegal for some time. Granted, it's possible that at some point in its distant history, parts of Oklahoma were underwater, and it's fortunate that any whales stranded by the receding oceans in the last millennium remain protected. A little parched, perhaps, but protected nonetheless.

To be fair, it's not just Oklahoma that feels the need to protect whales despite not having an ocean. Nebraska and Kansas also prohibit whaling; Ohio prohibits whaling, too, but only on Sundays.

By the way, those in Oklahoma who find themselves pining for the days of the whales might choose to comfort themselves with a smaller swimmer, maybe a goldfish. Owning a goldfish is legal, as long as the fish is not carried in a bowl on a bus.

WHEN NATURE BITES!

Bat Battle

While most folks were unaware of this particular law, health officials at Grady Memorial Hospital in Columbus, Ohio, knew all about it—the rabies repayment law. This law provides anyone "injured by a rabid animal" the option to ask the county commissioners for help paying medical bills related to the bite. In 2000 the law was revised to increase the payment to bite victims from the 1929 level of $200 to $1500. This ended up being a good thing for David Froehlich.

Froehlich was repairing a house in Ostrander, Ohio, and was moving an empty roll of linoleum flooring when he felt something on his finger. According to press reports he thought it was a staple, but upon inspection, he saw a bat on his finger. He shook his hand to dislodge the critter and flung it into the yard. The Froehlichs recovered the bat and took it in for testing, and sure enough, it tested positive for rabies.

Froehlich's treatment cost $5000, and local health officials encouraged him to seek reimbursement from the county. Even though he was technically two days past the deadline for requesting payment, the commissioners noted that in 1928 an Attorney General's opinion allowed them to utilize their discretion to ignore the timeline and take some of the sting out of the hospital bill for bite victims.

Smelling Across the Line

Rabies is one of the more devastating diseases that can spread from wild populations to domestic animals. Numerous laws have been passed in an attempt to curb the spread of rabies, but wild animals are notorious for crossing state lines without having proper permits.

In Tennessee, elected officials felt the need to clarify the law on this matter. They passed law "Tenn. Code Ann. 70-4-208," which made it illegal to import skunks unless they were headed to "bona fide zoological parks and research institutions."

Violation of the law was a Class C misdemeanor. Not too serious, but certainly enough to raise a stink.

SOMETHING FOWL

Chickens Do the Wild Thing by the Book

Chickens in urban areas are becoming more popular in the U.S. Urban chicken coops are all the rage, and many look like they've been picked out of the pages of *Architectural Digest*. But chickens aren't completely suited to the privacy challenges of city life. On April 25, 2011, officials in Hopewell Township, New Jersey, unveiled Section 5-9, "Standards for Keeping Chickens."

Most of the language in the ordinance focuses on the usual restrictions such as minimum lot sizes to house chickens and the size of any given flock (that's six chickens per half acre, but you can add four more for each additional half acre). In Hopewell, it's an all-girl town in terms of chickens. Roosters, known for their boisterous behavior, are forbidden except for a specified visitation time.

That's right, there is a sort of conjugal visit law for roosters. They can drop by the coop and "fertilize" for no more than 10 days, per parcel. Not only that, but roosters can visit for only five days in a row.

It's not all a hen party, either. The chicken-keeping ordinance has a "disturbing the peace" provision. Chickens are not allowed to disturb the peace or quiet of a neighborhood by "creating a noise" across the residential property line continually for 10 minutes (or intermittently for 30 minutes), unless provoked.

No word on the fine for provoking a chicken.

Forks Up! Seriously!

No city in the U.S. claims to have more to do with chickens than Gainesville, Georgia. The city has a large number of poultry processing plants. There is even a chicken monument in the city; it's a huge pillar with a "life-size" chicken on top.

Needless to say, chickens are a big deal in the city, so much so that there is a law about how to eat one. In 1961, as a publicity stunt of sorts, an ordinance was put on the city books making it illegal to eat fried chicken with anything other than your fingers. Fried chicken was defined as "a culinary delicacy sacred to this municipality, this county, this state, the Southland and this republic."

In 2009, Ginny Dietrick, 91, was celebrating her birthday at a café when she was busted by the police chief. Fortunately, she was immediately pardoned for the crime of "improper poultry consumption" by the mayor who "happened" to be in the restaurant. A friend in Gainesville set up the prank, and Ginny was quickly ordained an Honorary Georgia Poultry Princess.

Dietrick said in all her 91 years, this was her first run-in with the law other than a parking ticket.

Get a Coop

Chickens have become part of many urban landscapes. City dwellers in Austin, Texas, even have an annual "Chicken Coop Tour" in which some of the fanciest places you could imagine parking a hen are opened up for review throughout the city.

However, not every city welcomes hens with open arms. Here are a few of the restrictions on live poultry keeping:

- In Scituate, Rhode Island, elected officials found it necessary to place at least one limitation on residents who raise chickens. No one is allowed to keep a flock of chickens in a motor home in a trailer park. Maybe one or two is acceptable?

- Cumberland, Maryland has no restrictions on motor home coops, but chickens are not allowed in hotel rooms.

- In Illinois, you can have hens, but if they insist on cackling, there may be a slight issue. Cackling hens must be 200 feet from the nearest residence. So either keep them quiet or move them away from the neighbor's house.

- Lawmakers in Lewisville, Colorado, take a much harder line on fowl. Chickens are not allowed in the city at all; however, residents can have as many as three turkeys.

And for Sunday Dinner, We're Having Ham

Chickens put in a hard week. There's all the egg laying, the early-morning rooster calls, the endless worm search. Then there's wondering about the whole "Who's for dinner?" aspect of life in the chicken coop. It's nice to know that at least in Columbus, Georgia, even the chickens get a day off. Citizens are not allowed to cut off a chicken's head on a Sunday.

Free the Blue Chicks!

Kentucky is known for its Kentucky bluegrass, which have a blue flower head (if allowed to grow to their natural height of two to three feet). Bluegrass music sprouted from the imagination of songwriter Bill Monroe, a Kentucky native, who changed the tempo in the instrumentation of country music. In no time, a new genre of music had taken hold.

But how about blue chicks and indigo bunnies? Well, in Kentucky, despite their clear affection for the color blue, turning an animal blue—or any other color, for that matter—is against the law. To be specific, KRS 436.600 sets out the rules on animal coloring in quite serious detail:

> *No person shall sell, exchange, offer to sell or exchange, display, or possess living baby chicks, ducklings, or other fowl or rabbits which have been dyed or colored; nor dye or color any baby chicks, ducklings, or other fowl or rabbits; nor sell, exchange, offer to sell or exchange or to give away baby chicks, ducklings or other fowl or rabbits, under two (2) months of age in any quantity less than six (6), except that any rabbit weighing three (3) pounds or more may be sold at an age of six (6) weeks. Any person who violates this section shall be fined not less than $100 nor more than $500.*

Clearly there have been quite a few pastel-colored farm animals making their way into Easter baskets, only to be abandoned by their child caretakers after they return to their more natural color.

Chicks for Sale?

For cuteness, it's tough to beat baby chicks. The yellow fluff, the cute little eyes, the harmless pecking. However, along with ducklings and baby rabbits, chicks can become unloved after Easter is over. In Destin, Florida, no one can set up shop on the side of the road and either give away or sell baby chicks, ducks and rabbits or even offer them as prizes.

Pet shops, however, can set up sales in front of their stores. Even if they are selling baby Easter pets.

FOR THE BIRDS

Don't Bully the Birds

Throwing rocks at wildlife is not a nice thing to do, but generally it's not against the law. In Indianapolis, Indiana, you are allowed to throw a stone or other missile at a bird if it's in "self-defense." Those sparrows better watch out!

REPEALED
Quick—DUCK!

Until 2006, crows and starlings in Michigan spent the better part of their lives dodging bullets. That's because until that year, when this law was repealed, folks in that state were paid a bounty for every crow and starling they killed—they received 10 cents per crow and three cents per starling!

Birds, Listen for the Bell

Bird lovers are often in conflict with cat owners. Cats, beloved when they dispose of rodents, suddenly become criminals when they raid bird nests in the spring.

It seems that the bird lover lobby is a force to be reckoned with in Cresskill, New Jersey. In that city, all cats have to wear bells to warn birds. According to the American Society for the Prevention of Cruelty to Animals (ASPCA), some studies show that the bells are quite effective at warning birds; other studies indicate cats somehow manage to catch feathered prey even with the bells ringing. In Cresskill, erring on the side of caution, every cat must wear three bells.

THE BUNNY TRAIL

The Long-eared Ones Are Worth 50 Points!

While it's tough to imagine, at one point in time there were bunnies in New York City (the furry kind, not the scantily clad ones in magazines). When the city was just beginning to make the transition from farmland to skyscrapers, there were those who encountered a challenge while traveling along the trolley car rails. Rabbits.

The rabbit population was apparently considered a significant problem since someone thought it was a good idea to shoot rabbits from trolley car. Given the number of individuals who might be waiting to catch a trolley car and would prefer to board one without the threat of being shot at by an errant bunny hunter, lawmakers decided it was best to make it illegal to shoot a rabbit from a moving trolley car.

However, if the trolley car stops, the rabbits might want to think about scattering...

Is that Bunny Wearing a Snorkel?

They must have some extremely talented rabbits in Kansas. Not only can they procreate with incredible speed, corner with a skill that a racecar driver can only envy and deliver Easter eggs with a wiggle of their nose, but they can also swim.

In Kansas, lawmakers have made it illegal for hunters to shoot at rabbits from motorboats. Sailboats, though, appear to be fine.

DISTRACTING URBAN ANIMALS

Backseat Monkeys?

People tend to think of distracted drivers as a recent phenomenon, and a whole spate of laws focused on prohibiting cellphone use in cars have cropped up around the country. But ask any mother who has had a car full of hungry toddlers, and she'll tell you there are more distracting things in a backseat than chatting with a friend on a cellphone.

Still, one backseat distraction undoubtedly trumps them all—a gorilla. Perhaps that's why it's against the law in Massachusetts to have a gorilla hanging out in the back seat.

Usher! I Can't See Past the Gentleman's Mane…

It's a hot summer day and you decide to catch a movie. And chances are you want to see the movie with a friend with an appreciation for the wild action sequences.

You know, like your friend, the lion.

However, if you happen to be catching a flick in Maryland, taking a lion to the movies is strictly prohibited by law. Tigers are not mentioned specifically, nor are mongoose, which seems to be a terrible oversight.

Across the mountains in Wyoming, the concern about movie theaters wasn't lions, but hats. Moviegoers aren't allowed to wear a hat that would obstruct the view in a public theater. A similar law is in place in Columbus, Georgia and West Virginia.

HUMANE TREATMENT REQUIRED

Does This Cage Make Me Retain Water?

Here's the scenario: you're in Florida and you have a pig. It's in a cage. The cage is a little snug, but you figure it's probably fine. Then you get the news. This little piggy got knocked up! You may now be in trouble because in Florida, the cage for your pregnant pig must be large enough for the pig to turn around.

Have you ever seen a pregnant pig turn around? That piggy is going to need some room to maneuver.

It's not clear why only pregnant pigs are special. No other pregnant farm animal is protected by the law. And in the case of this law, it's not merely some oddball law added in during a legislative session. This law is in the state constitution, right in there with freedom of speech, lawful assembly and trial by jury.

Hawaii Is for the Birds

The University of Hawaii has 16 different birds that frequent the campus, including Myna birds, zebra doves and red-crested cardinals. They are common in Honolulu and seem to be quite revered because in Hawaii, it's illegal to annoy birds in a public park. It is not illegal, however, for the birds to annoy you or steal a cracker off your picnic blanket. Consider yourself warned.

Be Nice to All the Animals

Sometimes the odd part of a law is not the law itself, but how it defines terms. This is the case in an anti-cruelty law in Tennessee. In the definitions section of the law, it notes that the definition of a dumb animal includes "every living creature."

So be good to one another—dog, cat, worm and human alike!

Love Thy Neighbor

The right to be treated kindly is extended to the four-legged residents of Utah. In 1979, the state defined what is and is not acceptable when it comes to animal treatment: it's against the law to annoy, disturb, tease or irritate animals confined to their owner's property. It's also against the law to molest the animals. Animal service or law enforcement officers are exempt from this rule. The law doesn't state what is and isn't allowed should an animal be roaming the streets.

Merciful Execution?

It's a sad fact of life, but there are times when it's necessary for the authorities to put an animal down. Whether it's because of illness or abandonment, communities have used this method to control their pet populations for generations. That said, we do pride ourselves on being a civilized society. So it may shock you to know that at one point in Michigan's history, electrocution and high-altitude decompression chambers were used to euthanize animals. Thankfully, in 1919, a law was passed forbidding anyone from killing an animal using either of these gruesome and painful methods.

CATTLE GUARDS

We'll Have to Take the Toll Way

Any cattle trying to get through Chico, California, will probably have to take a hard right around the town. It's against the law for cattle, horses, mules, hogs, sheep or goats to be herded along public streets or sidewalks.

Get Your Hands Off That Udder!

Several laws in Texas focus on keeping cows safe, secure and in the right hands. In Temple, anyone with a cow in tow might want to have ownership papers in their pocket because cattle thieves can be hanged on the spot.

Up the road in Texarkana, it's illegal to milk someone else's cow—even if you're doing it because you have a late-night latte emergency.

In Austin, it's still illegal to have wire cutters in your pocket. The law goes back to the days when cows and other livestock were kept behind wire fences, and a sure way to expand your herd was to snip a few spots, mix your cattle in and claim there was no way to tell what cow belonged where. These days, wire cutters in Austin would be more likely used to trim guitar strings, not cut fences.

Proactive About Cow Pies

Keeping control of cow pies is a full-time job for any rancher. But New Hampshire decided somewhere along the way that highway crews shouldn't have to deal with all that manure on the roadways. Therefore, all cattle that cross state roads have to wear some sort of device to gather the cow pies before they hit the asphalt.

It's hard to imagine the effort that would go into designing such a device, let alone the full-out rodeo experience of affixing it to a moving cow.

Close the Door, or Else

Keeping track of livestock in Wyoming is a big job. Ranches are huge, and livestock have a tendency to wander off, which is why it's critical to keep all gates and fences closed. In fact, it's part of cowboy etiquette to close a gate if you're the one who opened it.

But etiquette is not enough. Closing a gate behind you is so critical in the state that if you don't do so, it could cost you $750, particularly if the gate is in an area where the fence surrounds a private road, river, stream or ditch.

Look Out for Your Livestock

Farmers in North Dakota need to mark their livestock and ensure their neighbors know their herd just in case one of their cows goes astray. If a cow wanders into your neighbor's field, and that neighbor honestly doesn't know who owns it and can't identify the owner after checking brands and going through all the official channels, your neighbor can take possession of the cow. It's finders-keepers for strays in this state.

Limits to Livestock Possession

In 1979, it was still acceptable for folks living in some Utah communities to keep a cow on their property. But there must have been some concerns about the practice since the state enacted a bylaw that year limiting the number of cows a family living within the city limits could keep on their property to a single heifer. In addition, the family must hold a permit from the County Health Department, and any cow-related paraphernalia, including feeding and milking equipment, has to be inspected by the authorities.

Mooooo-ve Over

Drivers need to keep their eyes peeled for any four-legged creatures wandering about on Wisconsin's roads and yield, at all times, to their movements. If that herd of cattle you've suddenly noticed is under the care of a handler, it is that person's responsibility to open the roadway up to vehicular traffic.

PARTICULAR TO PACHYDERMS

Can Someone Card that Elephant?

Some people really know how to throw a party. Manuel de Garcia de Texada in January 1810 placed an ad in the local paper of Natchez, Mississippi, indicating that he was hosting a live elephant show. However, it appears that even a live elephant show in 1810 needed more excitement. According to local legend, the elephant found some alcohol and drank it.

There's no story as to what happened afterwards, but one can imagine that a drunken elephant was deemed to be a bad idea. So bad that the city decided an ordinance was necessary to prevent other elephants from following suit and showing up in town drunk and disorderly.

Technically, elephants are allowed to get drunk. But they have to stay off the streets.

Elephant Ordinances

There must have been more elephants wandering around outside of zoos and circuses in the U.S. back in the early 1900s since lawmakers in Tulsa also felt compelled to step into the fray, so to speak. It's illegal to have an elephant in downtown Tulsa (drunk or not). There is no law against having an elephant in the suburbs, fortunately.

Virginia, Minnesota, is more flexible about pachyderms. Elephants can't be parked on Main Street, according to law, but as to the rest of downtown, there are no restrictions noted.

Hitch Up Jumbo, Ma!

Draft horses are the second strongest land mammal. They can pull literally a ton of weight for a short distance. Generally that's plenty of pulling power for any cotton farmer and his plow.

But someone in North Carolina wasn't satisfied with mere horse power. While there is no news report on a pachyderm causing havoc in cotton fields, it does seem like the kind of problem you'd want to prevent—especially when you were dealing with P.T. Barnum. According to press reports, the famed publicity king would often hitch an elephant up to a plow right next to the train tracks when his circus train rolled into town. It's unclear if this caused considerable damage or if it was considered too dangerous, but lawmakers in the state went on to prohibit elephants from being used to plow cotton fields.

RAGIN' CAJUN CRITTERS

That is *My* Alligator

It's not clear how many alligators there are in Louisiana, but it appears that at least some of them have owners. The state has a law against the "misappropriation or taking of an alligator."

The concern isn't merely the taking of the alligator intact. It's against the law to "to deprive the other permanently of the alligator, the alligator's skin, or a part of an alligator." The alligator doesn't even to have to be alive—dead alligators are also covered by the statute.

Taking someone's alligator, alive or dead, is a serious crime. In fact, getting convicted of alligator stealing can land a thief in jail for 10 years and cost them thousands of dollars.

Fans of alligator-skin boots might want to keep their receipts handy!

Crawfish Rustlers, Look Out

Crawfish boils are a staple of Cajun cuisine in Louisiana. The phrase "sucking heads" comes from the practice of pinching the head of the cooked crawfish to suck out the salt and spicy juices.

Given this affection for crawfish, it may not be so surprising that in Natchez, Mississippi, it's against the law to steal someone's crawfish.

How someone identifies a particular crawfish as his or her personal crawfish is not clear in the law. But the penalty for taking another person's crawfish is the same as it is for taking someone else's alligator.

BEE NICE!

State Troopers and Honey Bees

Bees, as many people know, get to a point with their hive where things get crowded and it's time to move on. This swarming activity usually means a large, dark cloud of buzzing and stinging bees rises and starts looking for new real estate. However, swarms, and perhaps even individual bees, had to stop by the vet's office before crossing the Kentucky state line. The law reads that all bees entering Kentucky must be accompanied "by certificates of health, stating that the apiary from which the bees came was free from contagious or infectious disease."

This law appears to have been aimed at commercial beekeepers who provide their bees as pollinators for farms and orchards. It's a sort of job protection bill to protect the local hives from the out-of-state bees. Still, any non-native bees buzzing in without their itty-bitty papers probably did all they could to avoid the state troopers.

Hive Control

Kentucky isn't the only area concerned with errant bees. In Kirkland, Illinois, bees are not allowed to fly over the village or down any of the streets in town.

Presumably law enforcement in the city is equipped with really tiny handcuffs.

THE DOMESTICATED SEGMENT

No Speak, Fido!

Dogs have come under some serious restrictions in Fort Thomas, Kentucky. Dogs, as well as domesticated animals in general, are not to disturb "public health and comfort." Of course, health and comfort covers a good deal of territory, but a few specifics are outlined in the law:

☛ Animals are not to have an offensive odor or stench.

☛ Pets are not to make noise that can be heard outside the home in an "excessive, continuous or untimely manner."

☛ Animals are not to "molest passersby or cars."

Therefore, owners with a yappy dog with a tendency to roll around in roadkill, yap at 2:00 AM then make amorous moves on the legs of passersby may want to whip out their checkbook—violation of the ordinance will result in a fine.

Canines Confined to Stairs in California

Dogs always seem anxious to rush through doors, but citizens need to be a bit more cautious in Glendale. Dogs are prohibited from riding in elevators unless they are leading a blind person.

Reading Is Ruff

It's against the rules in Cathedral City, California, to bring your dog to school, unless the dog is a police dog or service dog.

Sandy Paws Prohibited—Sometimes

Dogs in Myrtle Beach, South Carolina, can't drop by the beach whenever they feel like it. The city has several restrictions relating to canine beach visitors on the city's Ocean Boulevard. Dogs are not allowed on the public beaches or boardwalks from 9:00 AM to 5:00 PM from May 15 to September 15—which is basically tourism season—unless the dogs are official assistance animals or working with law enforcement.

It's not worth trying to sneak your dog to the beach, either. You can be arrested and the dog will be impounded.

In fact, dog owners can't even walk their dogs on the right of way of Ocean Boulevard in a 34-block area. This restriction starts in March and ends on the last day of September.

So Much for Being Pet Friendly

It's a no-no to take your pet to work in Juneau, Alaska, if you work where food is prepared and sold for human consumption. It's also against the law in that city for your pet to follow you to work if you work at a barbershop or beauty parlor.

Can't We All Get Along?

Dogs and cats have never been known for their peaceful co-existence, short of certain comic strips. However, in Barber, North Carolina, things may have been getting a little out of hand. Elected officials passed a law forbidding fights between dogs and cats.

It's possible that only organized fights are the target of the law, but citizens who observe a flick of a tail and hear a warning bark may want to alert the authorities.

Second-hand Smoke Goes a Little Too Far…

There are a whole host of laws protecting people from second-hand smoke. Studies show that children exposed to smoking can experience increased incidents of any number of breathing ailments. Workplaces, even entire cities, are now "smoke free."

However, only one community has found it necessary to protect a certain member of a household. In Zion, Illinois, it is against the law to give lit cigars to dogs, cats and other domesticated animals kept as pets.

Presumably unlit cigars are fine, but cigarettes and chewing tobacco could be trouble.

Smile at that Dog, Mister

Dogs are very attuned to physical cues. Experts at reading body language, a dog knows exactly who is most likely to sneak a treat under the table at a dinner party.

But these perceptive creatures can also read faces and aren't thrilled when they're taunted. That may be the reason citizens in Oklahoma aren't allowed to make "ugly faces at dogs." Doing so can result in a fine or jail time.

Man Bites Dog

When a man bites a dog in Paulding, Ohio, it's not just news, it's legal—if the biter is a police officer and the dog was barking.

Only a police officer is allowed to bite a dog to stop the animal from barking, which is probably a sensible precaution.

The biting police of Paulding might want to take a trip to Northbrook, Illinois, where it's illegal for a dog to bark for more than 15 minutes at a time.

Going to the Dogs

Lawmakers in North Dakota have an interesting way of deciding when a dog has become a public nuisance. According to the nuisance laws in that state, "Any dog that habitually molests a person traveling peaceably on the public road or street is a public nuisance."

However, "habitually" molesting a person doesn't necessarily mean the dog in question will be apprehended or its owner fined—at least not immediately. Once identified, a dog owner will be notified that a complaint against the dog owner has been filed. If a second complaint is made to the authorities, the judge can summon the dog owner to court. If the judge hearing the case decides the dog in question is indeed a nuisance, that judge can "order any peace officer to kill and bury the dog." The complainant must cover all costs incurred during the dog's execution unless the owner of the animal is known. In that case, the dog owner is expected to cover the costs.

What Goes in Must Come Out

Picking up after your dog should not have to be legislated; however, in South Bethany, Delaware, elected officials found that standards of good dog keeping were not enough. Thus, it's the law that all people walking dogs have to carry poop bags with them at all times. Caught empty handed when nature calls to Fifi? Get ready to dump $100 into the city coffers.

REPEALED
Pooping

Dealing with dog poop is a fact of life for any canine owner. However, in Cuyahoga Falls, Ohio, dog poop laws are really strict. Starting in 1980, a council ordinance was in place that prohibited "defecation" in the city by any animal, including dogs.

It's unclear how such an ordinance was enforced on the squirrel and possum population, which are notorious for thumbing their noses at attempts to constrain their activities. City officials repealed the ordinance in 2002.

Scoop that Poop *Now*

Cerritos, California, has no patience for poop procrastinators. City officials don't care if it's dog poop, chicken poop, cow poop or horse poop—the poop has to be picked up within seven days of its appearance on the scene.

The goal is to keep the fly population in check since any exposed poop is a breeding ground for flies.

Stick to Fetch and Sit

Chaser, a famous border collie, has demonstrated a comprehension of over 1000 words. Scientists at Wofford College in South Carolina even conducted a three-year experiment and found Chaser could comprehend the names of 1022 toys and would retrieve them from a separate room with 90-percent accuracy. In fact, Chaser was even better at putting words with objects than her handlers. According to MSNBC, "Sometimes the dog did better than her handlers, who reportedly had to write the names on 1022 toys to recall them correctly."

It's a good thing Chaser doesn't live in Hartford, Connecticut, where it's illegal to "educate" dogs, no matter how famous it makes the pooch. Whether the education refers to dogs like Chaser or simply to obedience school was not clear in our research. However, if it is still against the law, many dog trainers in Hartford could be in big trouble.

That Time of Year

Some might say love is in the air when Mother Nature kicks in the hormones and our formerly docile and predictable canine companions become anxious for a rendezvous with members of the opposite sex. Other people with less tolerance for the ebb and flow of such natural urges consider dogs in heat as a nuisance.

Members of Grand Forks, North Dakota's town council would likely opt for the second definition. To contain problems that could occur from such a situation, dogs in heat are not allowed to enter that city's off-leash dog park. Another good reason to go the "spay and neuter" route!

Get a Room! Or a Dog House! Or Something!

To say animals follow their instinct when it comes to matters of libido is putting it mildly. However, any animal caught mating "in public" near a church, school or bar are in violation of the law in Delaware.

It's unclear if water hoses are to be used to break up the violators.

Two's Company, Three's a Violation

Dog and cat lovers may want to steer clear of Bartlesville, Oklahoma. People (and oddly enough, corporations too) are limited to two adult cats and two adult dogs outside a residence.

However, you can have as many *inside* the house as long as each animal has a rabies vaccination, there's no "nuisance or health hazard" and the animals are well taken care of in the house.

Crazy about cats? Fancy felines? Love the sound of purring in the parlor? If so, you need to keep your kitties to three in Dudley, Massachusetts. And the fine is nothing to quibble over—it costs $100 per day for that fourth cat.

However, with a $50 residential kennel license, you can add an additional cat. According to the *Huffington Post*, the three-cat limit was inspired by Mary Ellen Richards and her 15 cats. Richards was quoted as saying she was moving to a more "cat-friendly" community.

Keep It Down, Kitties!

McHenry, Illinois, has several interesting ordinances in the Municipal Code, one of which includes section six that prohibits the ownership of lions, tigers, apes or monkeys. As well, any other animals that its citizens own are not allowed to caterwaul for more than 15 minutes.

★ ★ ★

Horse Power
(and Other Equines)

*Back in the day when horses were the primary
mode of transportation, many laws were in place
to try to keep order among the manure. After
all, these 1000-pound animals could trample the
populace if people did crazy things like suddenly
open umbrellas or drive down the street in one of
those weird wheeled contraptions—that is, cars.*

*We've included some golden oldies
from the horse days of long ago.*

GIDDY UP!

I Said WHOA!

Horses are known for their tendency to periodically ignore their riders and drivers. This may be why lawmakers in Washington, DC, felt it was necessary to insist on a certain safety device on all horsedrawn wagons.

Each vehicle pulled by horses was required to have an "effective brake." This is an acknowledgment that a shout of "Whoa!" is not always effective.

The Iron Horse, or Iron-deficient Horse

Horses, as any equestrian will tell you, have a fondness for chewing on various objects. They can chew up wooden fence planks in no time, giving beavers a real run for their money. Some horses are even escape artists, having figured out how to untie knot and unlock "horseproof" latches on gates and doors.

In Marshalltown, Iowa, though, horses must have had a thing for fire hydrants. A horse caught eating a fire hydrant was breaking the law. Not to mention a few teeth.

Gag Your Nag

In Pocataligo, Georgia, horses aren't allowed to neigh after 10:00 PM. It's not clear exactly how you can keep a horse from neighing, short of gagging it, which would probably bring on the wrath of several animal protection authorities.

Did You Get the Plate on that Horse?

Picture the scene: you're trotting your horse down a road, minding your own business and obeying all relevant traffic ordinances when you suddenly turn a corner and BAM!—you hit and kill a pedestrian. In Hortonville, New York, the law reads: "The rider of any horse involved in an accident resulting in death shall immediately dismount and give his name and address to the person killed."

Presumably this information is for use in the next life.

Keep it Quiet!

Horses startle easily. And when they startle, they run amok. And when the hooves come a-poundin', you better be a-running. In Pattonsburg, Missouri, their "revised ordinances" in 1884 state that no person was to "hallo, shout, bawl, scream, use profane language, dance, sing, whoop, quarrel, or make an unusual noise or sound in such a manner as to disturb a horse."

Gives a whole new understanding to the term "quiet little town," doesn't it?

Stick to Love Notes, Romeo

Along the same lines, West Union, Ohio, made it against the law for any male person to make "remarks" or even "whistle at" any woman riding a horse.

Fort Collins, Colorado, outlawed boys on horseback from winking at girls on horseback. Once on the ground, though, look out!

RWI—Riding While Intoxicated

Drinking and driving did not first emerge as a problem with the invention of the automobile. In 1913, Massachusetts found it necessary to outlaw drunk horseback riding. Given the strong startle reflex of horses and the lack of coordination brought about by drinking too much alcohol, it seems likely that RWIs were often accompanied by a few broken bones.

Absolutely No RWM—Riding While Married?

In Wakefield, Rhode Island, it's against the law for married men to ride a horse on Sunday. Maybe it was to keep the guys off their horses long enough to give their wives a shot at riding around town.

Enjoying the View

Mules are well known for their ability to climb safely, and in Massachusetts, this skill served them well. So many mules were on the second floor of buildings that safety precautions had to be put in place. No mule is permitted on the second floor of a building unless there are two exits. This is presumably because when a mule doesn't want to move, not much will make it budge. And that would cause a safety hazard, to say the least.

No Jury, No Judge

It's not surprising that tolerance for horse thieves is very, very low in the capital of horse country. In Kentucky, if someone steals your horse, you can hang him or her immediately. And, perhaps most disturbingly, police are not allowed to interfere.

Forget the Picket Fence

Some laws are darn right practical. In Bismarck, North Dakota, every home had to have its very own hitching rail, whether the owners had a horse or not.

I'll Have a Whiskey for My Mare and Me

In Temple, Texas, people are forbidden from riding their horse and buggy through the town square. Still, it's worth riding into town on a saddle. Folks can ride horses into a saloon.

We've Heard of a Tub of Lard…

Horses are not allowed to sleep in bathtubs in Budds Creek, Maryland, unless their rider is in the tub with them.

That's gotta be one heck of a big tub.

RUMORED
Beauty Is in the Eye of the Rider

Whatever you do, don't ride an "ugly" horse in Hartsville, Illinois—it's against the law. Riders, fortunately, are not held to the same standard.

Dim Lights Mean No Sale

Most people have heard the expression "You shouldn't look a gift horse in the mouth." The saying comes from the fact that you can learn a great deal from looking at a horse's teeth, such as its age, any bad habits it might have (like chewing on fire hydrants), and so on. This might be why the good people of Wellsboro, Pennsylvania, felt the need to enact a law prohibiting the buying, selling or trading of horses after sunset, possibly because lamp light around barns wasn't common yet. An exception could be made if the sheriff gave permission. A similar law was in effect at one time in Schurz, Nevada.

The Origin of Tail Lights?

Horses see pretty well at night; their owners, however, are as blind as bats. Clearly concerned with the potential for collisions, elected officials in Sutherland, Iowa, passed a law restricting the number of horses allowed on the street in the evening. To be on the safe side, the horse also needed some sort of light attached to its tail. Tail lights are also required in Texarkana, Texas.

Get that Mule a Bucket

There's an old saying that you can lead a horse to water, but you can't make it drink. Apparently mules are a different story. In Wynona, Oklahoma, it's illegal to let a mule drink from a bird bath. It's also illegal to wash clothes in a bird bath, in case anyone decides it's a good option after all that mule riding.

In One End and Out the Other

Horses, as well as cows, produce a great deal of manure, and the management of manure can become a full-time job. Given how much of the more metaphorical manure that is shoveled in Washington, DC, you might find it funny that, technically, manure is not allowed to be dumped in the "more densely populated areas of the District" without a permit from a health official.

Down the street in Boston, manure can't be kept in any building other than a stable. And only two "cords" of manure are allowed in the stable. Manure can't be left in the street, and moving it requires a permit. A cord of manure weighs a little more than three tons, so a bulldozer should probably be ordered.

Sorry, You'll Have to Walk

Unless it's a parade, no one is allowed to ride an animal or ride in an animal-drawn wagon down any street in Derby, Kansas. The chief of police can give prior written consent, but even then the consent will be for a particular person on a designated street during certain hours *and* under supervision of the police department.

There is something odd about a place named Derby forbidding the riding of horses down the street. But a conviction could cost the rider $100, so it seems best to keep your horse at home.

DRESS FOR THE GALLOP

What Are You Wearing?

Many horse-related laws seem to focus largely on what women riders are wearing while riding.

☛ In McAlester, Oklahoma, it's against the law for a woman over 235 pounds attired in shorts to be seen on a horse in a public place. Hear that ladies? Just get down to 230!

☛ In Upperville, Virginia, a married woman can't ride a horse if she's wearing "body-hugging clothing."

☛ Instead of banning certain outfits, city officials in Riverton, Wyoming, came up with a reasonable precaution. Women who wore bathing suits while on horseback had to be escorted by two police officers or had to carry a club. The law must have caused some consternation because it was later amended: "the provisions of this statute shall not apply to females weighing less than ninety pounds nor exceeding two hundred pounds."

☛ Then there's the funny little typo in Wolf Point, Montana's law that no horse shall be allowed in public "without its owner wearing a halter." Do they even make halters for men?

☛ And finally, in Omega, New Mexico, women on horseback must wear corsets, and physicians are required to inspect every woman riding by. Hopefully this kind of doctor visit doesn't require a $20 co-pay.

OF HOOF AND HIGHWAY

Keep it on the Track

The practice of finding a clear, open stretch of highway and putting the pedal to the metal apparently has a long tradition in the United States. So much so that Rhode Island found it necessary to pass a law prohibiting horse racing on a highway. The law, which carries a fine of $20 or 10 days in jail, also covers "testing the speed of a horse."

If pulled over, riders in Rhode Island might want to have an inventive excuse, such as someone opened an umbrella and spooked the horse.

Honey, Pull Over and Get Out the Wrench

When horses and automobiles shared the road, it made for a pretty chaotic scene. Horses were not so thrilled with the loud, smelly, metal monsters coming at them. In Pennsylvania, law-makers believed in sensible precautions.

Any motorist who spotted a team of horses coming toward him had to get busy. First, the driver had to pull well off the road. Then he needed to get out his camouflage blanket and completely cover his vehicle. If the horses looked at all nervous, the vehicle driver had to disassemble his car, hiding the parts from view.

Hey, Is that a Bottle Rocket? Must be a Car Coming!

Another sensible precaution borne of the intersection of livestock and automobiles in Pennsylvania (perhaps responding to the issue of individuals tired of taking apart their cars) was that drivers who were out at night on country roads were required to stop every mile and send up a rocket, wait for 10 minutes, then con-tinue driving. The idea was that the rocket would alert ranchers to clear the road of livestock.

The Laws of Nature and Man

Mother Nature is notorious for completely ignoring lawmakers. But that doesn't stop authorities from trying to rein her in anyway.

MAINTAINING CONTROL WHERE NONE IS POSSIBLE

Holding Back the Water

The Arkansas River is prohibited by law to rise higher than the Main Street bridge in Little Rock. While it's unclear who will have to serve time if Mother Nature opts to flood the place, it seems like a noble attempt to intimidate the river into staying within its banks.

That's One Big Rock, Sisyphus

The story of Sisyphus, the man who was doomed to roll a huge rock up a hill over and over again, could never have taken place in Boulder, Colorado. That's because it's against the law to roll large boulders on the streets of Boulder.

It's a law with a nice symmetry to it, don't you think?

Pest Control

Most people would agree that mosquitoes are a pain in the butt—and in the arm and leg and any other part of the human anatomy. But Minnesota lawmakers took their frustration with the bothersome bug a step further than other states when, in 1999, they officially declared mosquitoes a "public nuisance," whether they are "disease bearing" or not. Furthermore, the "Land of 10,000 Lakes" has deemed it "advisable and necessary for the maintenance and betterment of the health, welfare and prosperity" of its residents to aggressively rid any and all corners of their state of the pests. To that end, officials are mandated to spray, fog or otherwise attack any pool, ditch or other area providing the right conditions for the incubation and hatching of mosquitoes.

A Weed by Any Other Name Might be Illegal

Weeds are the bane of every avid gardener. They invade carefully tended yards with a fury, they spread on the slightest breeze and they grow so quickly that overnight you can have a yard full of uninvited flora, ready to overrun your expensive lawn.

Which may be why it's illegal to grow thistles in your yard in Maryland. It's unclear if it's only illegal if a person purposely plants them, or if they just spring up after it rains.

It's Great to be Green

Minnesota lawmakers in 1851 appeared to have a sensibility toward maintaining adequate green space. A statue passed that year encouraged landowners with property bordering a public road of any description to cultivate what they called a "live fence"—a permanent border created by a hedge, bushes or other suitable greenery. State residents were expected to respect this living border at all times. If anyone was discovered to have "wantonly or maliciously" damaged these live fences in any way, they were in big trouble. If found guilty of such a crime, the perpetrator could face a fine of $100, a jail term of 30 days, or both, if the court deemed it appropriate.

Leaf it Alone!

There are numerous laws against messing with or picking up bits of the outdoors and keeping them for yourself. Some of these laws make sense, such as the prohibition against taking rocks from the Petrified Forest National Park, but other laws seem a little odd.

- **Seaweed:** It's illegal to pick seaweed off the beach in New Hampshire at night. That's the ocean's job, thank you very much. During the day, you can haul off as much as you want.

- **Sand:** A city ordinance in Rehoboth Beach, Delaware, protects the sand on the beach. No sand is permitted to leave the beach on your body, shoes or clothing. It's not clear if sand inspections are done at all exits from the beach. Shake that towel, visitors!

☛ **Trees:** In Columbus, Georgia, you'll need to find a less damaging way of expressing your love on trees. It's illegal to carve your initials on a tree, even if the tree is on your property.

☛ **Ginseng:** From April to September in North Carolina, you can't go on a ginseng dig on someone else's lawn. That law has been in effect since 1866 when, we presume, ginseng digs were all the rage.

☛ **Cacti:** Their prickles might have protected them from all kinds of predators in the past, but these days, cacti need a lot more than protruding spikes to keep from being damaged by thoughtless saboteurs. In fact, some folks think cacti make for good target practice. No worries, though—Arizona's Native Plant Law prohibits anyone from cutting or collecting native cacti without a permit. In light of this legislation, shooting at them willy-nilly is definitely frowned upon.

☛ **Bluebonnet:** Texas is quite proud of its state flower, the bluebonnet. In fact, it's a rite of passage among young children in the Hill Country area to stand in a field of bluebonnets, often on the side of a busy highway, and get their parents to take photos of them. There's even a wildflower farm outside Fredericksburg, Texas, that specializes in bluebonnets. But what makes all this fuss a bit ironic is that, in many places, the bluebonnet is considered a weed, and it's considered illegal to pick a bluebonnet on public land in Texas. However, it's okay to sing the song written for the bluebonnets called "The Bluebonnet." It's worth noting that most violators of this particular law are about five years old.

☛ **Flower tossing:** In Kentucky, you are not to throw flowers at a public speaker. Violating the law could land you in a decidedly flowerless place for a year—jail.

Air Versus Tree

Usually, cities welcome tree planting, but in Blairstown, New Jersey, trees cannot be planted on a street side that might "obscure the air," which is a good thing since breathable air is at a premium.

Soggy Root Prevention

Florida puts restrictions on flowerpots. Yours better have a drain hole in the bottom, or it's considered a public nuisance by virtue of being a mosquito haven.

Don't Hurt the Rocks!

In Colorado, you are in big trouble if you disfigure or injure any rock "beyond normal use." Also under protection are trees, shrubbery and wildflowers in recreation areas.

That Plant Is Outta Here!

There are many horses in Norco, California, and horses will nibble on almost anything, even things that will kill them. One of those things is oleander plants. Oleander is one of the most poisonous of commonly grown garden plants, prized for their showy pink, white and red flowers. And it's against the law for anyone—people, corporations or public agencies—to plant them in the city.

Is There an App for Sunshine?

Controlling the weather has always been a dream of vacationers, farmers and chambers of commerce. While most people are willing to wait out bad weather, Texans are determined to do something about it.

Given that recent summers and persistent droughts have dealt a harsh blow to the state's citizens and agricultural interests, it's not surprising that Texas lawmakers have leapt into action. They established a grant for research into weather control. This is particularly ironic given Texas' official stance on global warming—basically, that the state's multiple refineries do not contribute to global warming.

★ ★ ★

I Do, I Don't and
the Spots in Between

*Relationships are complicated. And when couples
decide to dive in for the whole nine yards, marriage
is certain to get more complex in many states.
Whether it's the approval of the farm animals or
the requirement to carry through on rash promises,
the laws around marriage could convince some
couples to forego walking down the wedding aisle.*

PRE-MARITAL BLISS

Old Laws or Old Wives Tales?

Laws evolve over time. A community regulation that made sense in the early 1900s doesn't necessarily fit well with all segments of today's society. Take dating, for example. We all know it wasn't that long ago when "premarital sex" was a dirty word, and young woman caught in a compromising position could ruin her reputation, and that of her family, forever. So although it might be surprising to some readers, one source stated that unmarried couples in Idaho who had premarital sex and had their naughty deed proven to the authorities, sometimes had no choice but to abstain for as many as six months—because that's how long they could find themselves incarcerated for.

Honor System

Although sexual abstinence might not be a philosophy that other North Americans generally adhere to, staff and students of Brigham Young University (BYU) in Utah overwhelmingly embrace abstinence. That institution's "Honor Code" explicitly states that chaste and virtuous behavior from its staff and students affiliated with the university is expected at all times. In part, that behavior includes abstinence from any form of sexual misconduct, including "sexual relations between members of the same sex" and "all forms of physical intimacy that give expression to homosexual feelings."

A 2011 news article on the issue of premarital sex among college students cited statistics collected in 1954. The numbers at that time suggested that only 14 percent of students in the entire country were having sex before marriage—it appears more recent statistics are not available. What is available is an annual record of the number of reports on potential violations: between "1.5 percent to 3.5 percent of students were contacted by the

Honor Code Office about potential violations." Other Honor Code violations at BYU include visiting a dorm room belonging to a member of the opposite sex and wearing revealing clothing, such as sleeveless, strapless or backless tops.

While many of these rules might appear strange or out of the ordinary to some, they are borne of a specific faith tradition. BYU's Honor Code has struck a chord with at least one other institution of higher learning. According to the same 2011 article, the University of Texas in San Antonio adopted several sections of BYU's Honor Code in 2008.

Looking for Love? Look Again

Trying to tie the knot with some special girl? Back in the day when there were no Internet dating sites, single men had to get creative. A little too creative, perhaps. In Tranquility, New Jersey, a person was prohibited from distributing handbills while on horseback as a "means of advertising for a wife."

Honoring Women

Wedding vows are taken very seriously in Michigan, and so is protecting the honor of a lady. In what should be called the "gentleman state," men who try to "seduce" or "debauch" an unmarried woman of any age will be charged with a felony, and if convicted, face a five-year jail sentence. If the convicted man is diligent about paying his dues for the crime, he might get off with a scant $2500 fine, but if he doesn't pay up within a year of the time the offense was committed, it's off to prison for him!

Be Careful with Those Promises, Boys

In Mississippi, a man has to stick by his word, especially when wooing members of the opposite sex. Seducing a woman over 18 years of age by promising her marriage and then skipping out on the "I do" is considered a crime, punishable by five years in jail.

There are a few conditions that have to be met before a conviction can be made under the law. The woman has to have been "of previous chaste character," and the testimony of the woman alone is not enough to convict. It's not clear whether the declaration of marriage must be witnessed or if the previously chaste nature of the woman must be proven somehow.

Either way, it seems wise for Mississippi men to be careful not to propose marriage lightly.

South Carolina has a similar law, although the potential jail sentence is only one year. Once again, South Carolina puts a premium on virginity—there's no crime if a man promises marriage, but the woman was already "lewd or unchaste."

The court can also stay all proceedings if the couple gets hitched either before or after a conviction.

MARITAL BLISS?

Young Love

Most states in the U.S. require that couples planning to get married must be 18 years of age or older. Nebraska is the exception—you have to be 19 in that state to marry without parental or legal consent. Generally, state officials will accept parental consent for 16 and 17 year olds wanting to tie the knot. If you're under 16, you're pretty much out of luck, although some sources suggest that if a baby is involved, there are states that will consider allowing the exchange of vows with or, in these cases, without parental consent.

Proxy Marriage

Age requirements for the solemnization of marriage vows might be stumbling blocks for some young lovers anxious to tie the knot. But what if you and your chosen live miles—maybe even continents—apart?

Marriages that take place when one person is absent from the ceremony, and is represented by another person, are called a "proxy marriage." This kind of marriage, though unconventional, isn't altogether uncommon in the U.S. At times, a proxy marriage is desirable when the bride or groom is in the military, or if a travel restriction is imposed on one of them. Proxy weddings are sometimes also the way to go when the bride or groom is in jail!

Despite the fact that a proxy marriage is recognized as a legal union in all states, only four states in the country will allow it to take place within their borders: California, Colorado, Texas and Montana. Of course, saying "I do" is only the first step in the official marriage process.

Many traditions around the world require a marriage to be consummated through the act of sexual intercourse or, in gentler words, by "becoming one flesh." In the Catholic Church, a marriage that hasn't been consummated can be annulled. Usually, doing a tango between the sheets is a requirement most couples are more than happy to comply with. That said, it might be a little frustrating to have to prove you've done the deed. How does a person prove such a thing?

Proving you've consummated your marriage is exactly what's required if you're marrying a foreigner and that person wants to immigrate to the U.S. Although the United States Citizenship and Immigration Services (USCIS), along with the various branches of the federal government and "all U.S. States and territories, and all foreign nations which recognize U.S. marriages," recognize a proxy marriage as valid as soon as it has been officiated, the marriage must be consummated before it will be "recognized for immigration purposes. This is known as the 'Consummation Requirement.'"

According to the Marriage by Proxy website, proof of consummation can be given in several ways: by "providing copies of visas, airline tickets" and "photographs," for example. That the two lovebirds were able to get together to consummate their marriage begs the question, of course, about why they had to organize a proxy marriage in the first place?

Double Proxy Marriage

But what if both partners can't be at the specified place and time to formally say "I do" in front of their chosen administrant? In this case, a couple is looking at what's called a "double proxy marriage." Why, you might ask, would someone book a wedding with an officiate at a place that neither partner is able to attend and where two strangers stand in for the bride and groom? Good question. Perhaps both are serving overseas in separate military stations? Or maybe both are in jail—in separate states. In either case, a double proxy marriage is recognized in all 50 states. But only one state in the country allows this kind of marriage—Montana.

The same consummation requirement stands when it comes to immigration laws as they pertain to a double proxy marriage. Somehow these two long-distance lovers need to get together for at least one conjugal visit to appease the authorities that their marriage vows have been signed, sealed and delivered.

I Don't Think He's Bright Enough

Some people believe couples are crazy for getting married in the first place, particularly given the tax penalty and rate of divorce in this country. Getting married is no small affair in the smallest state in the U.S., and being crazy in love may not be a defense for a poor choice in a marriage partner. In Rhode Island, the law states that any marriage where either person is an "idiot" or "lunatic" is considered null and void.

Till Death Do Us Part

While not actually punishable by death, folks committing adultery in the state of Michigan are in serious trouble. Not only do they face the wrath of the spouse they've wronged, but they are also guilty of committing a felony. In addition, unmarried men who've become enamored with a married woman are "liable to the same punishment," although the details of said punishment are unclear.

RUMORED
I Don't Know, Honey, the Pig Looked at Him Funny

Getting married is a huge commitment, and wise folks know that when you are getting married, you aren't merely getting hitched to the person you love, you're also getting hitched to a whole new family. Lawmakers in Raleigh, North Carolina, realized that for a marriage to last, more than one person's views on the union should be taken into consideration.

Before a Raleigh man asks a woman to marry him, he has to subject himself to inspection by "all the barnyard animals" on the woman's family property "to ensure a harmonious farm life." It's unclear if disapproving livestock were ever quietly hastened to the dinner table.

Talk About Micromanagement

There appears to be much debate on the following alleged law, and the verdict is out on the length of time it may have been on the books, but according to several sources, it was unlawful for a woman living in Michigan to visit the local beauty salon to have her hair cut without her husband's approval. One has to wonder what Michigan law thinks about joint bank accounts.

Where Property Rights and Marriage Collide

North Carolina was a slave state before the Civil War. As such, the state had many laws on the books dealing with the day-to-day life of slaves. However, their rights after the war were subject to considerable interpretation.

North Carolina lawmakers felt it necessary in 1866 to pass a law validating marriage between slaves: "Persons, one or both of whom were formerly slaves…shall be deemed to have been lawfully married."

It took another 90 years for the state to pass a law validating interracial marriage.

What Did You Say?

Texas is a common-law state when it comes to marriage, which means no formal ceremony is required to be considered hitched with somebody. One of the ways a couple can be considered married is by publicly introducing someone as their husband or wife three times.

This makes bars in the Lone Star State a potential minefield of matrimony.

Kissing Cousins Is One Thing…

In 1879, the pickings for potential spouses were pretty slim in North Carolina. A detailed description of "degree of kinship" was set into the marriage code, specifically stating:

> …the half-blood shall be counted as the whole-blood: Provided, that nothing herein contained shall be so construed as to invalidate any marriage heretofore contracted in case where by counting the half-blood as the whole-blood

*the persons contracting such marriage would
be nearer of kin than first cousins; but in every
such case the kinship shall be ascertained by
counting relations of the half-blood as being only
half so near kin as those of the same degree of
the whole-blood.*

Thank goodness they cleared that up.

A Common Conundrum

According to the National Conference of State Legislatures,
a common-law marriage is defined as a marriage where two
people "agree that they are married, live together, and present
themselves as husband and wife." No official ceremony is necessary. According to the 1990 edition of *Black's Law Dictionary*,
all that matters is that there must be "a positive mutual agreement, permanent and exclusive of all others...and an assumption
of marital duties and obligations."

Of course, not all states recognize this type of common-law marriage as valid, and in some states that validity has changed over
the years. For example, Idaho did acknowledge common-law
marriage as a legitimate civil union at one time, but in 1996 that
recognition was revoked. According to Idaho's statutes, marital
consent between two adults must be followed by "the issuance of
a license and a solemnization as authorized and provided by law."

Lawmakers did agree, however, to acknowledge that common-law
marriages that took place before 1996 were still considered valid.

★ ★ ★

Health, Hygiene and Napping

Many laws are focused on preventing us from injuring ourselves or others by dashing about life in an unsafe manner. This section covers a few of the more peculiar ways our nation's laws aim to keep us safe from harm—or at least keep us smelling good.

AVOIDING INJURY, ONE WAY OR ANOTHER

Put Down that Knife; It Won't Do You Any Good

Who among us as children didn't hold a thermometer to the heater to convince our moms we had a fever? Or stayed home from school or work by faking a bellyache? Well, in Alabama it appears there was a problem with employees taking the faking a step further. Section 13A-14-1 is a law targeting those who would "maim" themselves to get out of work.

Referred to in popular culture as "the law against stabbing yourself for pity," the actual law makes it a felony to disable oneself to avoid performing a legal duty. The law is designed to not only stop people from ducking out of work but also to stop all pity parties. It reads that any person who would "so injure himself with the intent to avail himself of such injury to excite sympathy or obtain alms or some charitable relief" is, in fact, guilty of trying to get out of work for no good reason.

The law was passed in 1923, and it's difficult to know what "legal duties" the citizens of Alabama were trying to avoid by maiming themselves. So close up the faker pity party, folks—it's a felony.

A Little Too Late

There are some laws where any punishment for breaking them will not likely deter people from the act the law aims to prohibit. Not because the activity is so much fun people will do it anyway, but because it would be almost impossible to mete out the fine.

This is the case with one law in New York City. It's illegal to jump from the Empire State Building.

Two questions spring to mind. First, does this mean it's legal to jump from other buildings? Second, given that falling a certain number of stories carries the ultimate penalty, what exactly is the point of a fine or jail time?

The Womb, The Tomb and The Elevator

Another behavior subject to strict New York regulation is riding in an elevator. Elevator etiquette is no small thing in a city where people are routinely shoved together like sardines. Psychologist Layne Longfellow noted that "There are only three times in our lives that we enter a small, windowless, enclosed space that has no ready exit: the womb, the tomb, and the elevator. The elevator is the only one we share with strangers."

The elevator etiquette law is straight out of kindergarten hall behavior: riding in an elevator in New York, people are not to speak to one another, they must keep their hands folded and look toward the door. Some New Yorkers theorize the law came about because early elevators were prone to accidents, mostly cable jams. People would tend to flail about so the law was intended to keep people relatively still and balanced in what were not always safe journeys between floors.

No Peeking!

In Washington State, it's against the law for just anyone to use "X-ray, fluoroscopic, or other equipment or apparatus employing roentgen rays" as ways to find a fit for that perfect shoe. Exactly how these tools make it easier to fit shoes is a mystery! The only people who can legally view the bones in your feet are specific licensed health practitioners, so presumably if these professionals sell shoes as a sideline, they might legally employ such methods. This law was passed in 1973 and updated as recently as 1990— the term "podiatrist" in the original law was expanded to "podiatric physician and surgeon."

Can You Hear Me Now?

It appears there's a hierarchy involved in almost everything. Life is made up of committees and boards and the meetings these organizations demand. It would be interesting to learn the story behind the formation of an advisory group in Iowa for the specific purpose of licensing and regulating hearing-aid dealers. Strict rules also dictate who can sit on this board. According to this law, five board members are named: three who are licensed hearing-aid dealers and two who represent the general public. The hearing-aid dealers must have a minimum of five years' experience in their field, with no less than two of those years serving in Iowa. And no more than two of the three licensed dealers can belong to the same company.

Overdone?

In our quest to obtain the golden glow we call a suntan, we sometimes have to pay the price—it's known as a sunburn. Although most of us have a general idea of how our skin will respond to being outdoors on a hot summer's day, we never really know for sure. That's why doctors advise the use of sunscreen—to protect us from sunburn and the subsequent complications that sometime arise from too much sun exposure.

Perhaps it was this pursuit of a bronzed complexion without the dangers of sun exposure that may have, at one time, drawn men and women to tanning-bed facilities. These days, however, most people are aware that tanning beds can pose as many health risks as natural sun.

Even though all the dangers related to sun tanning appear to be common knowledge, Iowa State law legislates that all cosmetic tanning establishments must post signs warning clients of all the risks involved in using their equipment. Signs must be "in a conspicuous location" so anyone entering the establishment can see it. All customers must also be given their own written warning statement.

Still, with all that information giving patrons 1001 reasons why they should not strip down to their skivvies and slide under the lights in these glowing coffin-like beds, tanning studios do a booming business. Weird or what?

Mandatory Quarantine

It is against the law to walk around anywhere in Washington if you have a contagious disease. Even the common cold will keep you at home and in bed with a cup of hot tea—one doesn't have to worry about calling in sick to work with a law like this on the books. This rule extends further to include any sick pets you might own. If Fido is under the weather, he'll also have to forgo seeing any of his pet friends until he recovers. No doggy walks for him!

DECENT EXPOSURES

Breast or Bottle?

Isn't it funny how sex and violence permeate every corner of today's society, even extending to television and billboard advertising, and yet something as pure and innocent as a woman breastfeeding a baby in public can be a subject of hot debate? In fact, breastfeeding in public was once considered by some people to be indecent exposure, and the practice was outlawed in Washington. It was an emotional, highly volatile issue that, many argued, threatened women's rights. And in 2001, the issue of breastfeeding was specifically addressed in the state's indecent exposure law, clarifying that "the act of breastfeeding or expressing breast milk" was not considered indecent exposure.

Once a Week, Kids, It's the Law!

A weekly Saturday-night bath was pretty common during the 19th and early 20th centuries since, at that time, the work week was longer. Many people worked at least a half day on Saturday around the turn of the century. Even so, preparing a bath was a lot of work back then, so Saturday became the bathing day of choice. After all, Sunday was a day of rest—and church.

In Barre, Vermont, elected officials thought the locals might be tempted to skip taking a bath one week. It was decreed that all residents had to bathe every Saturday night, possibly in order to clear the air for church on Sunday, which would give the word "pew" an additional ironic twist.

It's hard to know what was happening in the middle of the week in Cheyenne, Wyoming, but one thing is for sure, folks weren't spending time getting clean. It was against the law to shower on a Wednesday.

RUMORED
No Feet, Please

Ornately carved claw-foot tubs have recently made a bit of a comeback and can be found in homes restored to their historical glory. But claw-foot fans better think twice before buying one in Kansas City, Missouri. Someone may have gotten a little creeped out by the animal-like paws on some bathtubs, or maybe there was some long-lost political significance to having paws on a tub. Whatever the reason, lawmakers in Kansas City outlawed animal paws on tubs.

You Want to Check My What?

If you're passing through Detroit and yearning for a hot, sudsy bath, but you don't want to shell out the cash for a hotel, you'll be pleased to know city ordinances are pretty strict when it comes to ensuring the bathhouses in that community are disease-free. Owners can turn away a potential patron for something as simple as a sore throat. And even though employees can't help a member of the opposite sex, they are all expected to undergo a physical examination to confirm they are free of communicable diseases.

At Least They Don't Need Sunscreen

Nothing is more relaxing on a hot summer night than a dip in a swimming pool. If you live in an apartment complex in Clemson, South Carolina, though, you'll want to hop out of the water by 11:00 PM, otherwise you'll need a certified lifeguard present if you want to swim between 11:00 PM and 7:00 AM.

Thinking of sneaking in the water anyway? Think again. Skimping on the lifeguard will cost you a fine of up to $500 and possibly 30 days in jail.

BODILY FLUIDS AND... SOLIDS

Spit into the Wind

Spitting has a long history of coming in and out of favor. Back in the Middle Ages, spitting was considered a necessary act, although you had to spit under the table and not on it. According to an "etiquette manual" from 1729, "You should not abstain from spitting, and it is very ill mannered to swallow what should be spat."

Then a little thing changed all this spitting tolerance—tuberculosis. By the 1800s, spitting became garish, and the spittoon business was born. Generally, spittoons have gone the way of the buggy whip, but you can still find them in some places, including the Supreme Court, where each justice is provided with one.

In Baltimore City, Maryland, it's against the law to spit on the sidewalk, but spitting on the street is fine.

Yes, You Can Spit Here

One habit from the turn of the century has not disappeared, although only one town has a law that accommodates it. In El Paso, Texas, spittoons are required in saloons, churches, hotels, banking rooms, halls of assembly, stores, markets and railroad depots. Not only are they required, but also there must be enough of the right kind of spittoons to serve the needs of spitters.

Restrooms Are for Employees Only...or Not

When you gotta go, you gotta go. And in Illinois, they gotta let you go. Known as the Restroom Access Act, Statute 410 ILCS 39 requires retail establishments to allow customers with real emergencies to use the employee-only facility, with a few caveats. The customer has to have some sort of medical condition that limits his or her ability to hold it, so to speak, or if an ostomy device is involved. In addition, three or more employees must be working at the time the customer requests use of the facility, the restrooms must be safe and secure (although cleanliness is not a factor) and no other public options must be available.

Go Ahead, Flush!

The government of Wisconsin is prohibited from "either directly or indirectly" prohibiting manual-flushed urinals in the state. It's not clear why a government might outlaw manual flushing; perhaps it was once instituted as law in an effort to curb the spread of bacteria? In any case, the "Flushing Devices for Urinals" law directs officials at the health department to "take steps to encourage the use of manual" flushers.

Hold it Until You Get Home

Myrtle Beach is a major tourist destination in South Carolina, attracting some 14 million visitors each summer, even though the area's population is only 27,000. The city has many beautiful parks and public spaces, many with attractive water features.

It's important for visitors to note the difference between "water features" and "water closets." It is illegal to pollute the waters with any substance, liquid or solid, of any "fountain, pond, lake, stream, bay or other body of water." This would include urine.

Alamosa, Colorado, is slightly clearer on the matter, noting that urination in a public place or within public view is illegal. This includes streets, alleys, schools, "places of amusement," playgrounds and common areas of buildings.

Public pooping is also a no-no.

Whistle While You Work, But Keep it Quiet in the Privy

Public toilets are generally a single-function kind of space, but in Washington, DC, lawmakers felt it was necessary to set some limitations. Patrons of public restrooms in the District must be careful not to whistle.

Gotta Go?

Urination and defecation might be natural bodily functions, but if you opt for the local bush to relieve yourself while out for a stroll in Tempe, Arizona, it could cost you $300. That's the maximum allowable penalty for not going before you leave home!

Don't Dump Your Poop

Bets are on that most of us have had to make do in one way or another when it comes to adhering to the call of Mother Nature. However, if you've had to cut open a plastic bottle to serve as a portable toilet, don't just open the car door and deposit it on the side of the road. If you do, you'll be breaking Oregon state law, and if you're found guilty of throwing or otherwise leaving "a container of urine or other human waste on or beside the highway," you could face a fine of up to $250. Now that's what you might call an expensive bathroom break.

As odd as that restriction is, the law also prohibits singing, skating, dancing and swearing. Patrons should also not bother the restroom attendant, particularly with show tunes.

No Squatting Allowed

The official rules at Washington's Seattle Center Campus put a whole new spin on pooper scooping. The school's rules state that urinating or defecating anywhere other than in a bathroom is absolutely prohibited. No kidding?

Keeping it on a Roll

If you need to make a pit stop in Hermosa Beach, California, you'll be happy to know that it is required by law for all "toilet rooms" to have toilet paper. Plus, the facilities have to be clean. Might be worth going out of your way on your next road trip!

KEEP IT CLEAN

The Sky Is Falling?

In case you haven't caught on to all the fervor over how important it is for the environment that we don't litter, you might want to keep reading. It's illegal to drop litter from a plane when flying over Juneau, Alaska. Anyone convicted of breaking this law faces a $200, $250 and $300 fine for first, second and third violations, respectively. Not sure how one might go about identifying the aircraft and/or person responsible for committing such an act, nor how that individual could manage to do something like this without being sucked into the ether and, ultimately, the litterbug's heavenly home.

Water Bottles Are a No-No

In 2010 in Concord, Massachusetts, lawmakers made it against the law to drink water out of plastic water bottles. The goal of the law is to reduce waste of plastic and to increase awareness of the impact on the environment of the millions of empty bottles.

Clean-shaven Women Only

Before the advent of electrolysis and laser hair removal, shaving was the only option for women who were determined to rid themselves of the hair on their legs and under their arms. But only in Carrizozo, New Mexico, is it actually against the law for women to appear in public unshaven. Yes, New Mexico may be known as the "Land of Enchantment," but for women it's a hairless kind of enchantment.

Do You Have a License for that Facial Hair?

There was a time when beards were seen as a something worthy of control by law. In Massachusetts, an old ordinance declared goatees illegal—unless the goatee wearer paid for a license to wear one.

Save the Pavement!

Citizens in Hermosa Beach, California, are mighty protective of their pavement. It's considered against the law to pour salt (rock salt or common salt) on the pavement.

But the law is not limited to salt. The prohibition extends to oil, petroleum, kerosene, benzene, oily substances or liquids, acid, chemicals, broken glass or other substances that "might damage pavement."

Some Things Are Just Tacky

Minnesota's lawmakers frown on folks scattering tacks on public sidewalks. Why, you might ask, would someone deposit this kind of potentially prickly litter on a path where people trod? Good question. It appears this "law" is just one in a series of bullets falling under a statute addressing nuisances "Affecting Peace, Safety and General Welfare." Along with the "no tacks allowed" rule, this law prohibits a wide assortment of possible grievances, including a warning against selling something on public or private property without the owner's permission being "conspicuously displayed on the item for sale," and stockpiling any "old machinery, junk, furniture" and so forth on one's property.

Managing Your Health

It appears that having a sore neck after 6:00 PM isn't a good idea in Minnesota, especially if you typically seek out the services of a registered massage therapist. That's because no one in that state is allowed to go into a massage parlor after 6:00 PM or before 8:00 AM. No exceptions. And if customers or patrons so much as enter the premises between 12:00 AM and 6:00 AM, they are guilty of a misdemeanor. So much for working overtime!

Don't Even Pretend!

Wisconsin's Elmbrook School Board prohibits smoking on school property. No surprises there. However, should you "place any tobacco product in [your] mouth," you're breaking the law as well, which means you can't hang an unlit cigarette from your lip on your way to the public sidewalk for a smoke. The same law applies to chewing tobacco.

Put Down that Marker!

Few foods have a more wholesome reputation than milk. From lactation to latte, drinking milk has been one thing you could count on being a healthy part of your day. Of course the days of milkmen dropping off glass bottles are long gone, along with accusations that they might be delivering more to lonely house-wives than dairy products. However, in Massachusetts, there has been some intrigue in the milk aisle.

It appears that a gang of marauders went on a rampage with some sort of marking devices and did the unthinkable: they defaced milk cartons. Lawmakers quickly swept into action, making such acts of lactose larceny illegal.

Keep Your Feet Out of Our Fountain

Nothing is more effective at cooling a person on a hot summer day than taking a dip in a nice, clean body of water. But citizens in Rockville, Illinois, need to think again before availing them-selves of the cooling waters of public water features. The law doesn't allow anyone to stick their foot, hand or any other part of their body in a Rockville-owned fountain or pool. This includes wading as well, unless the pool was constructed and is operated specifically for swimming.

And if you do spot someone floundering in the middle of a non-swimming pool, don't toss anything to save him or her if that item could be considered debris, which would violate the second part of the law.

Fridge Leftovers

Before the advent of the avocado-green refrigerator, most major appliances were white enamel. They were termed "white goods."

As anyone who has visited a junkyard will attest, old appliances don't disappear—they clutter up landfills and are fairly hazardous to boot. In North Carolina, lawmakers have ensured that washing machines, stoves and refrigerators pay for their "funeral" expenses right from the start. Every appliance sold includes a $3 tax, which helps fund the safe disposal of the white good when its service life is complete.

RUMORED
Sweeping Ordinances

Cleanliness is next to godliness in the minds of lawmakers in Pennsylvania. The state has an actual ordinance on housecleaning. If that isn't bad enough, one law in particular makes it illegal for housewives to hide dirt and dust under a rug. No word whether a similar law exists for the lawmakers.

FLOSSING AWAY

Now, Bite This

While everyone would love to keep all their teeth for all of their lives, the reality is that throughout American history, some people have had to resort to fakery to keep a grin in place.

Nebraska has completely different concerns, mostly around issues of substance. That is, the material used to make dentures. Absolutely under no circumstances is leather to be used to make false teeth. This seems like sage advice, really.

Things get pretty personal in Massachusetts. There is a law on the books that requires couples to remove false teeth prior to engaging in…carnal acts. So much for a love bite!

Has Anyone Seen My Princess Toothbrush?

There's no question that dental hygiene is important, and still having your own teeth makes retirement so much more pleasant. Taking care of those pearly whites is a habit that starts when people are young, when most of the teeth they're brushing are going to fall out in a few years.

In Massachusetts, brushing those baby teeth isn't just a good idea, it's the law! Day-care providers must help children in their care brush their teeth. Parents with objections to day-care dental care can opt out; however, the tiny protests of the kids who don't want to brush are not protected under the law.

Who's Laughing Now?

Nitrous oxide, which is also known as "laughing gas" or "sweet air," is commonly used in dentistry as an anesthetic and an analgesic. Many dentists use it to calm patients who dread having their teeth worked on.

Called "laughing gas" because of the euphoric feeling it produces in patients, nitrous oxide can turn a trip to the dentist into a trip to wonderland. In Indiana, lawmakers have banned sales of nitrous oxide if the sole purpose of the sale is to, in effect, make people laugh.

Nix on the Nitrous

There are more than 100 laws on the books of Utah's Criminal Code addressing "Offenses Against Public Health, Safety, Welfare, and Morals." As with laws everywhere, there must be reasons for their formation, however obscure they might be, that stem from some point in the community's history. Utah's legislation relating to nitrous oxide addresses at least one of the four categories of health, safety, welfare and morals.

In 2002, the state legislature enacted a law against "abuse of nitrous oxide." For those of us who are not familiar with drug use, the idea of using this substance is, well, mind numbing. While the possession of nitrous oxide doesn't appear to be illegal federally, some states have instituted laws around its possession, sale, distribution and use. Utah has included this topic in their morality laws. In the state, it is against the law to "breathe, inhale, or ingest" this drug for the sake of intoxication and its subsequent potential mind-altering behaviors. The use of nitrous oxide is only legal when a licensed medical professional uses it for the purposes of "medical, surgical or dental" care.

Don't Breathe In!

If individuals can't get to the dentist for nitrous oxide in New Hampshire, they apparently avail themselves of another gas of sorts. Inhaling the exhaust of city buses in order to gain a feeling of euphoria is illegal in the state. So motorists should be warned to close those air vents and roll up their windows if they are stuck behind a bus!

SLEEP TIME

Don't Sleep on the Beach

The beach can be a relaxing place, and it can be tempting to catch up on your sleep. But it's not advisable to drift off to dreamland between midnight and 8:00 AM if you're in the town of Fenwick Island, Delaware. Taking a nap during the day is okay, but nighttime beach visitors are not allowed to snooze. In fact, people with a bonfire permit must start cleaning up by 11:00 PM to ensure they are off the beach by midnight.

Is That Guy Snoring? Book Him!

How convincing are you when you pretend to be asleep? Can you pull a blanket over your head and convince the world you have really nodded off?

Take care and don't try this on a park bench in Delaware. Not only are you not allowed to sleep on a park bench, but you aren't allowed to fake it either.

Presumably you can claim you were only resting your eyes. Or meditating. Or trying to figure out whether that shape in the clouds was a bunny or the Capitol building. Whatever you do, don't drift off!

Freedom and Other Sticky Subjects

The Constitution is an inconvenient document
for some lawmakers trying to rein in an unruly
populace. Fortunately the Supreme Court has
a certain affection for its unruly populace, resulting
in quite a few laws surviving perhaps only because
everyone is too embarrassed to bring them up.

CURSES!

What Did You Say?

Tempers can get heated in playgrounds and parks. Someone takes someone else's Frisbee, some kid swipes another kid's ice cream cone, a game of flag football gets out of hand. In Rockville, Illinois, it's best to restrain from cursing about the injustice of it all. According to Section 15-52 concerning "improper language or behavior," it's against the law to "use any profane or indecent language or behave in an offensive manner in any public park or playground of the city or upon the sidewalks adjoining any public park or playground."

It's unclear if the ban extends to music. Certainly, several modern musical selections could run afoul of this law.

Watch Your Mouth in Michigan

It used to be illegal in Michigan to curse in front of women and children. Generally these laws are on the books from a century ago and don't seem to be regularly enforced. However, they are still technically laws, and therefore are subject to use by local police. This was the case with the 1897 swearing statute.

A Michigan man who had an unfortunate canoe accident learned about the law the hard way. In 1998, while floating along a lake, he fell into the water fully clothed. The experience inspired him to let loose with all manner of profane language in the presence of women and children. Police arrested him and charged him with breaking the swearing statute.

The American Civil Liberty Union (ACLU), upon hearing of the case, fought the law on First Amendment grounds. Timothy Boomer, the soggy man in question, was convicted of uttering "a stream of profanities in earshot of a woman and her two children."

The court case, however, stressed that the law itself was unconstitutional because it violated the First Amendment right of freedom of speech, which, reflecting on many historical situations, was a philosophy that predated the law's institution. The law was overturned.

Cursing bans still continue in several states, although they seem to have escaped the attention of the ACLU and courts so far, gosh darn it!

Dads, Watch Your Tongue

Fathers are known for bestowing nicknames on their children. "Kiddo," "Sonny" and "Buster" have all been shouted out to offspring at one point or another. Unfortunately, not all the nicknames that fathers bestow are kind in nature. Sometimes a dad might call his son a name in an effort to use a form of reverse psychology. For example, "slob" for a messy son who fails to clean his room.

In Staten Island, New York, however, there is a restriction on parental name-calling. Fathers may not call their sons "faggot" or "queer" in an attempt to get them to act in a more "manly" way.

That's Rude—in New York, Anyway

If you live in one of the most densely populated cities in the country, there are many unspoken rules. There are rules about personal space, waiting in lines and hailing cabs. But some forms of etiquette are so critical they have been codified into law.

One such law falls in the category of inappropriate greetings. In New York City, you are not allowed to greet someone by giving him or her the "five-fingered salute," also known as "Queen Anne's Fan" or "cocking a snook." This is when you place your thumb on your nose and wiggle your fingers. The gesture may have been made illegal because in Britain it was a sign of contempt. Generally it's merely a joking insult these days, but international travelers should be cautious—in other countries the gesture is offensive and could get you into some trouble. So keep those wiggling fingers confined to the U.S.!

Be Nice, or Else

New York is not the only state trying to legislate to a more civilized society. Indiana has a law making "spiteful gossip" and "talking behind a person's back" illegal.

This approach is shared by Oakland, Florida, where gossip or spreading rumors is illegal within the city limits. In Oakland, it's considered a form of disturbing the peace, which, when you think of it, is a pretty apt description of gossip.

The Problem with Defaming the Court

Vermont has a law against saying mean things about the courts in the courts. In fact, a news report in the *New York Times* indicated how difficult this law is to fight. A defendant identified in the story as "Sutton" said something somewhat insulting about the court's inability to be impartial. The court convicted Sutton of violating Section 5072 of Vermont law, which makes it a criminal offense to defame a court. The defendant pointed out during his appeal that the judge should recuse himself because the judge couldn't exactly be impartial when he was the one being insulted. The conviction remained.

Keep Your Cool

Holding your tongue when someone cuts you off on the road is not simply demonstrating self-control. In Rockville, Maryland, it keeps you out of trouble. In that city, it's not only in playgrounds and sidewalks that you have to watch your tongue—cursing, swearing and using obscene language on the highway is also illegal.

GROUP ACTIVITIES

Associate at Your Peril

There's nothing like a good old-fashioned fight at city hall to throw the United States Constitution under the bus. The city council in Gould, Arkansas, was having a tough time figuring out how to deal with the city's back taxes. As is often the case in politics, factions quickly formed, and some members of city council found themselves not included in some meetings.

One councilwoman opined, "You couldn't just come in here and get with four people and decide you want to start an organization." Clearly unaware of a document known as the Constitution, the council proceeded in 2011 to pass an ordinance to forbid meetings without the entire council present. The Gould Citizens Advisory Council, which counted the mayor among its members, had been showing up at public meetings and was being critical of officials. Which is no fun if you're the targeted official.

The ordinance passed noted that neither "the Mayor nor city Council members shall attend or participate in any meetings with any organization in any location without City council approval by [a two-thirds vote]. The Gould Citizens Advisory Council…is hereby banned from doing business in the City of Gould."

And, to make matters slightly more unconstitutional, they added: "no new organizations shall be allowed to exist in the City of Gould without approval from a majority of the City Council."

The reality that the right to association is guaranteed by the First Amendment of the United States Constitution did nothing to deter the Council. "Pretty clearly, they go way beyond what is necessary or what is lawful," said general counsel Mark Hayes, with the Arkansas Municipal League, in local press reports.

"That's even what Gould's city attorney told the council. In return, members tried to fire him," noted one reporter.

Just meeting with reporters for interviews on the ordinance, members of the council were in violation of the town ordinance.

After a few weeks of controversy (and perhaps a lesson in Constitutional Law), the Council repealed the ordinance, realizing that taking on the First Amendment would be a little bit of an overreach.

Communist Connections

Listing their extra-curricular activities on a resumé is usually one way would-be employees can demonstrate their varied interests to potential employers. But if you are a member of the Communist Party in Nevada, it's probably not a good idea for you to mention that—especially if you really want the job you are applying for. That's because a law enacted in 1965, during the heat of the Cold War, allowed businesses to refuse employment to applicants with Communist Party connections. The Subversive Activities Control Board finalized the law "pursuant to the Subversive Activities Control Act of 1950," and although it's technically still on the books, it is in the process of being repealed.

Atheism in Vermont

Many laws in New England have puritan roots, and their very nature flies in the face of the United States Constitution itself. For example, in Vermont, it is illegal to deny the existence of God.

NATIVE AMERICAN RELATIONS

Pioneer Panic

Back in the days of the Wild West, relations with the Native American population varied greatly. In some areas, there was trade with indigenous peoples; in other areas the situation between whites and Natives was quite tense. The sighting of a single Native American was enough to send the local pioneers into a full-blown panic.

Various states had laws to provide cover for rather dramatic reactions to the appearance of more than one Native American at a time. These laws are still on the books but are clearly no longer enforced. At least we hope not!

Can I Have an Amen?

In South Carolina, adult males are required to bring a shotgun to Sunday church services to ward off attacks from "Indians."

No Slumber Raiding Parties!

In Columbus, Georgia, all Native Americans were required to return to their side of the Chattahoochee River every night.

Stick to Pairs

In South Dakota, if there were three or more "Indians" walking down the street, they were considered a "war party." That meant it was okay to fire upon the group.

Anyone Have Change for a Dime?

One little known fact about New York is the large number of Native American Indian tribes in the state. As tribes, they are exempted from many laws other residents have to deal with, including the New York City's eight percent parking tax.

It's unclear how this is handled in areas with meters.

Smoking with the Natives

New York state Native American tribes are also exempted from cigarette taxes since the tribes are considered sovereign nations, leading many tribes to set up special stores to sell tax-free cigarettes. After some legal challenges, the tribes have recently started making and selling their own cigarettes. Sales are substantial. According to the *New York Times*, "in the first six months of 2011, the state's Indian nations imported 9.6 million cartons of brand-name cigarettes."

DECENCY DEFINED

Keep it Zipped, Son

As Ozzy Osbourne found out, it is illegal to urinate on the icon of Texas independence—the Alamo in San Antonio. It was back in the 1980s when Ozzy was touring the U.S. Finding himself with a full bladder and a nearby building, he let it fly, so to speak. The arresting officer reportedly said, "Son, when you piss on the Alamo, you piss on the state of Texas."

Saggy Pants and Civil Rights

States across the nation want the youth of America to pull up their pants. The style of having sagging pants has annoyed so many communities that numerous laws have been passed in an attempt to prohibit the style. Because nothing makes something less appealing to youth than making it illegal, right?

Unfortunately for the anti-droop contingent, it's tough to write a law that meets constitutional muster. Still, it's an issue of such intense interest that cities as diverse as Riviera Beach, Florida; New Orleans, Louisiana; Memphis, Tennessee; and Flint, Michigan, have all tried to develop a workable law. Then-senator Barack Obama noted in an interview on MTV in 2008 that Florida's attempt to crackdown on baggy pants was a waste of time, but he added, "Some people might not want to see your underwear—I'm one of them." That year, the law was declared unconstitutional, but only after several arrests had been made.

In Dublin, Georgia, the mayor signed a bill to amend public-indecency laws to include anyone who "appears wearing pants or skirts more than three inches below the top of the hips (crest of the ilium) exposing the skin or undergarments." It's worth noting this is the first mention of sagging "skirts," as most of the other laws target strictly drooping pants. The city council also inserted their justification for the law. They were acting out of health concerns, specifically that "wearing sagging pants is injurious to the health of the wearer as it causes an improper gait."

First-time violators should be careful when reaching for their wallet. The first offence will cost you $25, but if you droop your pants again, the fine goes up to $200.

Heel-height Limits

The municipal code of Carmel, California, includes one restriction on shoes. No heels greater than two inches in height or with a base of less than one square inch are allowed without a permit.

Not many women in stilettos are being pulled off the city sidewalks in Carmel, but the law is on the books. It was the product of a concerned city attorney in the 1920s to defend the city from lawsuits stemming from high-heeled trippers on the city's sidewalks.

Permits for high-heel wearing are available for free at City Hall.

Turn Around and Face the Orchestra Pit!

Leave it to the fear of lawsuits to inspire some pretty weird laws. For example, concert hall owners were worried about slip-and fall lawsuits. Somewhere along the way that worry translated into laws prohibiting walking backward. In Greene, New York, people are specifically prohibited from walking backwards while eating peanuts.

Why peanuts? Why not pecans? Or bubble gum? Surely caramels would require even more concentration?

Port Allen Unfair!

Laws like the ones found in this book could drive people to protest. The right to protest is protected in the U.S. (until some municipalities claim it isn't); however, rules still have to be followed.

In Port Allen, Louisiana, two people can protest at the same time on a sidewalk, but they have to stay five feet apart from one another.

It's unclear whether this is to keep disagreements peaceful or to give picketers their own personal First Amendment space.

FLAGGED

Pledge Allegiance to Texas

Every school-age child in the United States is familiar with the Pledge of Allegiance, recited every morning across crackly speakers in classrooms. The pledge, formerly adopted by Congress in 1942, has been the subject of some controversy. It's been modified four times, and the most recent change was adding the words "under God" in 1954. Some religious beliefs frown upon pledging allegiance to anything outside of its faith.

In Texas, however, school children have to take it one step further. Every child in school pledges allegiance to the state of Texas in addition to pledging allegiance to the United States. The Texas Pledge, which is remarkably similar to the Pledge of Allegiance, was established in 1933. In 2007, the words of the pledge were also amended to add the words "one state under God."

Adding the words "under God" caused controversy, but as of 2012, they have withstood legal challenge.

Beware the Flag Pole Violation

Flags have always been much more than mere decorative bits of fabric. They are symbols that embody everything from patriotism to rebellion. After all, one of the most famous flags in the U.S. is the one first used by the U.S. Marine Corp during the American Revolution—Gadsden's Flag, or as it's more commonly known, the "Don't Tread on Me" flag that features an angry rattlesnake.

Given the clear historical precedent for flags to stir revolution, West Virginia's flag law makes sense, even if it is inconveniently unconstitutional. In the state, it's illegal to even possess, let alone display, any red or black flag. Black flags have been associated with anarchist movements since the 1880s, and pirate ships in the West Indies used both black and red flags when raiding ships.

Other states have had black and red flag laws, but they have not withstood court challenges. West Virginia's law, which extends to any symbols that indicate "sympathy with or support of ideals, institutions or forms of government, hostile, inimical or antagonistic to the form or spirit of the constitution, laws, ideals and institutions of this state or of the United States," remains on the books, ripe for constitutional challenge.

Standing Proud

The Stars and Stripes are a proud symbol of the USA, and the flag that bears the red, white and blue should be cared for with respect. It's common knowledge that citizens are expected to give proper care and attention to this nation's banner. The same is true for state flags; the "Desecration of the Flag" law, first enacted in South Dakota in 1939 and revised several times since, spells this out in considerable detail, in case anyone has any questions on the matter.

Of particular interest is the mention that respect for the flag must extend to any "flag, standard, or colors, or any part thereof, made of any substance and of any size *evidently purporting* to be the flag…" Even if a flag isn't an official flag but simply the loving efforts of a young student's school project, it merits the same respect. In that case, the flag, in any of its potentially great forms, enjoys a better sense of equality among its peers than most humans do!

REPEALED
Lawmakers Have to Learn How to Duck

Political speeches in Kentucky at one time were a protected type of speech. Protected from eggs and rotten tomatoes, that is. Kentucky law KRS 437.050 stated:

Any person who interferes with any person addressing a public audience within this state, who interrupts such a person, while speaking, by the use of insulting or offensive language or opprobrious epithets applied to the speaker or who attempts to interrupt or injure the speaker by throwing missiles of any kind at him shall be fined not less than fifty ($50.00) nor more than five hundred dollars ($500), or imprisoned for not less than one (1) year nor more than six (6) months, or both.

But in January 1975, the legislature decided they could take their chances without a ban. That was the year after Watergate, and it's possible a few folks felt they needed the full force of the First Amendment at their fingertips, rotten tomatoes and all.

The most prominent tomato tossing occurred in December 2009, when vice-presidential candidate and former Alaska governor Sarah Palin was the target of a rotten tomato. The incident happened at Palin's book signing held at a Barnes and Noble in Bloomington, Minnesota, for her autobiography *Going Rogue*. However, Jeremy Paul Olsen should have spent more time in the bullpen working on his aim. The rotten tomato landed on a police officer instead of Palin.

Minnesota doesn't have a "rotten tomato tossing law" so authorities had to settle for charging Olsen with disorderly conduct and assaulting a police officer.

Dining, Sort Of

Eating out is a great way to get out of doing the dishes but can be fraught with peril or, at a minimum, poor food choices. Here's a collection of laws that may convince you to just pop something in the microwave.

CREATIVE CULINARY CHOICES

Don't Mess with Texas Trash Cans

Texas has no problem with trash-talking, but when it comes to trash-eating, well, them are fighting words!

In Texas, eating your neighbor's (or anyone else's) trash without permission is prohibited. So if you suspect there might be a little something yummy in the Jones' garbage bag, take a minute and get a signed permission agreement before tearing it open.

Clearly, most raccoons and stray dogs in the state are unaware of the law.

Clean Your Plate—By Yourself

Diners in Memphis have the perfect excuse to use when keeping all that cherry filling to themselves—the Pie Law.

Most folks know that one of the key ways restaurants drive up the cost of a meal is by offering desserts on their menus. Even the most humble diner has killer dessert options for those who can't resist the fluff of a light meringue or the down-home smell of cinnamon and hot apple pie. Most times, patrons opting to share a dessert means the bill won't be padded.

Unfortunately, in these calorie-conscious times, ordering dessert and sharing it with your group is also seen as a precursor to a trip to a hospital emergency room because of food poisoning. You aren't allowed to share your pie in Memphis. And you even can't take home your pie leftovers. So dig in!

Drawing the Wrong Kind of Attention

Residents in Soldotna, Alaska, could keep manicured lawns and orderly yards and still find themselves being charged with allowing an "attractive nuisance." A full garbage bin, or perhaps even a well-stocked compost heap, might all lend themselves to the breaking of this law. That's because these items might attract a bear and, well, lawmakers in this city frown upon that kind of thing since a bear is no small nuisance. Not only is it a tad disconcerting for residents to have a bear wandering about, but it also costs a lot of money to relocate or capture the animal.

Roadkill—It's for Dinner!

There's hunting and then, for those with slightly less ambition and aim, there's roadkill. Every day, the roads of America are littered with the unfortunate results of vehicular Darwinism. Animals don't seem to quite make the connection that jumping out in front of vehicles is a bad idea.

But it does beg the question: what exactly are the rules around roadkill? What if you happen to mow down a nice-sized deer, and visions of venison sausage suddenly pop into your head? What can you get away with, and more importantly, where?

- ☞ If you're in Tennessee, you are in luck. Harvesting roadkill and eating it is perfectly legal. However, etiquette suggests letting your guests know if their meal has come from the store or the road along the way.

- ☞ If you're in Texas, drag the poor dead animal to the side of the road and leave it there for the fine folks at the Texas Department of Transportation to pick up.

- ☞ Maine doesn't mind if you grab the road kill. You just need to call the police, who need to tag it first.

- ☞ Illinois is fine with you collecting the road kill, as long as you weren't the one who did the deed. Basically if you saw someone hit the animal, or your cousin brings it to you, you can keep it, provided you report it to the Department of Natural Resources. Minnesota is of similar mind.

☞ Make sure you get your paperwork in order in Missouri. You have to have written permission to eat a deer that's roadkill. It's similar in Wyoming, where you have to get the animal tagged by a game warden.

☞ Wisconsin offers free permits to remove roadkill.

☞ Sometimes you'll find something dead that isn't roadkill, per se. If you happen to find a dead bird on your lawn in Conyers, Georgia, for example, you can't just quickly flick it on your neighbor's lawn. You have to dispose of it properly within 24 hours.

☞ And if you're in Galesburg, Illinois, don't toss the bird in your burn pile. It's illegal to burn bird feathers.

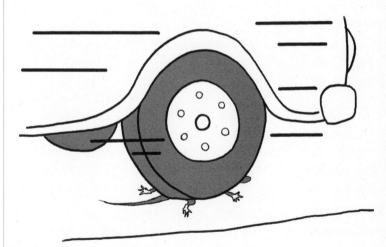

FAKE AND DISCARDED FOODS

Is it Butter?

Missouri takes butter very seriously. So seriously, in fact, that there is a law against yellow margarine. You can have yellow butter or white margarine, but not yellow margarine. Back in 1895, lawmakers were trying to protect local dairy farmers from the products of a cheap competitor who was adding yellow color to make the margarine look more appealing. It was the kind of law that was fairly common back in the day, but adding the yellow dye has been largely repealed around the world, including in Paris, France, which was one of the last holdouts.

It remains the law of the spread in Missouri, though.

Better Be Butter

Wisconsin's lawmakers take the threat of false advertising to heart, especially when it comes to their butter. "Students, patients, or inmates of any state institution" are to be served butter. Butter substitutions, like oleomargarine, are not allowed. The only exception to this rule is if the student, patient or inmate requires a butter substitute for health reasons. Restaurants are also forbidden from serving a butter substitute unless a patron has requested it.

The butter wars have a long history in the U.S., dating back to the 1870s when laws restricting sales and imposing strict rules about labeling margarine were instituted. Governments also imposed color bans and additional taxes to help consumers distinguish between butter and margarine and, it was hoped, protect the dairy industry. It appears the animosity between the two industries in Wisconsin, which is a leader in the country when it comes to milk, cheese and butter production, is still alive and well centuries later. If you are found guilty of serving a butter substitute in this state, you can be charged a fine of between $100 and $500. You could also face a term of up to three months in jail, where you can count on being able to slather real butter onto your mashed potatoes!

Bounce Your Pickle

When is a pickle a pickle? When it bounces! The true test is when a pickle is dropped one foot above an oak table and then bounces. At least this is the rumored law in Connecticut to test whether a pickle is a pickle. After we conducted a test (what we do in pursuit of truth!), it's clear that pickle bouncing is possible, but dribbling is out of the question.

Head Taster

Here's a law that school children everywhere would undoubtedly support. In Los Angeles, the source of all the food served in a children's camp has to be approved by the director of the camp.

This would mean, of course, that many directors would have to accept personal responsibility for the food and therefore have accountability for any mystery meat being served. In effect, this limits the ability of camp directors to rely on third-party vendors to avoid liability.

Keep Those Peels

Look like one too many people slipped on a banana peel in Mobile, Alabama. It's against the law for anyone to "spit or throw fruit skins, parings or peelings" on the sidewalk. But sidewalks are not the only restricted places. Public elevators, public buildings, theaters or halls and the walkways in public parks must also be peel free.

Buses are another forbidden zone for leftover skins. When in Mobile, carry a bag, fruit fans!

Special Delivery! Surprise!

Ordering a pizza for a friend could get you in trouble in Louisiana. Especially if you do it without letting your friend know. Maybe it all started as a college prank, or maybe some kid sent the governor a pizza he didn't want. Whatever the reason, there's a detailed set of rules about "unauthorized ordering of goods or services" in the state.

Here are the conditions that have to occur to be in violation of the law:

- ☞ The person getting the item didn't authorize it or live with the person who placed the order.

- ☞ The item is not a gift.

- ☞ The person getting the item has to pay for it.

- ☞ The person placing the order is doing so to be annoying.

Ordering a prank pizza will cost you up to $500, which doesn't even include the price of the pizza, and possibly six months in jail. That's a whole lot of penalty for a little misguided pepperoni.

And You Thought Banana Peels Were Slippery…

Recently waxed floors are the bane of slick-soled men and women everywhere. But an even greater danger in Glendale, California, was present—wax containers.

Wax containers shaped like small soda bottles often held sweet syrup, which was a popular candy product in the 1950s. Kids just bit off the top of the "bottle," sucked down the sugar water and went on their merry, sugar-hyped way.

Unfortunately, kids wise enough not to eat the wax container just tossed it to the ground, and according to the good lawmakers in Glendale:

> *The discarded wax containers constitute a hazard to pedestrians and make the sidewalks unsafe for foot travel because of the greasy and slippery condition resulting on the sidewalks. Several persons have fallen because of that condition. Such containers are a hazard to the health of the city because of the number of flies attracted to them.*

As a result, the council made it illegal for anyone under 18 to buy wax containers, putting the waxy soda bottles in the same category as malt liquor.

★ ★ ★

Taking Care of Business

Every industry from construction to accounting is carefully regulated to ensure it is following a whole host of laws. Some laws are designed for public safety; others seem to be a tad overprotective of the nation's businesses. A few of the more unusual ones are included in this section.

CONSTRUCTIVE LAWS

It's Illegal But Darn Impressive

Construction is a dangerous activity. Between the power tools and heavy machinery, safety is a constant concern. Fortunately, the elected officials in Massachusetts have established considerable safety protocols, one of which includes a prohibition on stilt walkers.

It is illegal to allow someone to use stilts "while working on the construction of a building." Stilts are actually quite common among drywall hangers, but in Massachusetts, they'll have to stick to ladders.

Lean on Me, But Not My Bricks

In Clinton, Oklahoma, when it has been a long day and folks are ready to take a load off, they had best opt for a park bench. Leaning on a building is illegal in that city.

Don't Injure Our Buildings!

New England is filled with historical buildings, so it makes sense that officials would be worried about keeping them intact. In Rockville, Maryland, Section 13-58 forbids the "removing or defacing buildings, fences; violation of section declared misdemeanor. A person may not deface, or injure or remove any fence, gate, railing, porch, building, or other structure upon public land, by writing, cutting or in any other manner within the corporate limits of the City."

Home, Sweet Home

Since 1989, the last Sunday of June has been known as "Log Cabin Day," although it has been around unofficially since 1986. That's when Virginia Handy and the Bad Axe Historical Society first hosted the day to celebrate the log cabin, a "symbol of humble origins in American politics since the early 19th century." The goal of log cabin day is to raise awareness of early American life—and to encourage owners of log houses to spend the day at their home and celebrate with a feast "in honor of the love of log cabins."

WEAPONS AT WORK

Keeping Explosives to a Minimum

Once again it would be pretty interesting to know the story behind this particular law in Billings, Montana. The city council decided to limit the weaponry at their meetings to include, but not limited to, bombs, grenades, explosive missiles, large caliber weapons, rockets, Molotov cocktails and silencers. Get caught with any of these weapons (and a long list of others) and it's a $500 fine or six months in jail.

The fact that a specific law about weaponry was needed is interesting enough, but that the prohibition is limited to city council meetings seems to leave a great deal of room for mischief, to say the least.

Keep Your Snowballs to Yourself

Back in the Middle Ages, nothing was quite as destructive as a good old-fashioned catapult. It could knock down walls, destroy fortresses and generally ruin someone's day.

Lawmakers in Aspen, Colorado, may have been greatly concerned that catapults were going to make a comeback. They prohibited anyone from aiming a catapult at a person, building, vehicle or public place.

The same law also prohibits firing a bow, blowgun, slingshot or gun. And, oddly, snowball fights are also illegal.

Snowman building, presumably, is still permitted, as long as no one loads the snowman into a catapult.

SERVICE INDUSTRIES

Cutting the Air

Barbers work in close proximity to one key sensory organ—the nose. As such, customers are going to be well aware of the scent of their barber. However, some barbers in Waterloo, Nebraska, may not have taken care when ordering off the lunch menu. Lawmakers felt it was necessary to forbid barbers from eating onions from 7:00 AM to noon.

If your barber takes an early lunch in Waterloo, you may want to bring him a mint.

Sit Back and Relax

Oregon lawmakers banned self-serve gas bars in 1951. Since then, it has been illegal for anyone to pump gas into his or her car in that state. However, it appears that motorcycles and boats are exempt from that rule.

Romantic? Or Just Dark?

Low lighting can set a mood, but if you're trying to order off a menu, a dark room could make it difficult. Any establishment that sells alcohol in Arvada, Colorado, has to have lights bright enough to allow patrons to read anything written inside.

Not for Auction

It is against the law for a person to "sell, dispose of or offer for sale" at public auction any "gold, silver, plated ware, precious stones, watches, clocks or jewelry" in Detroit, regardless if you own these items or are serving as an agent for someone else who does. Exceptions to this rule include retail and wholesale businesses and pawnbrokers.

Keep it in the Back

In University City, Missouri, you can have a yard sale. But not a frontyard sale. Not only that, but yard sales, even the ones held in backyards, can't go on for more than two days. So markdown those lawn tools early!

REPEALED
Feeling Lucky, Punk?

Ice cream can be messy, and the folks in Carmel, California, like a clean sidewalk. That may be why before 1986, selling or eating ice cream while standing on a sidewalk was prohibited.

Enter actor and Carmel mayor, Clint Eastwood. During his tenure, the law was repealed, making it a lucky day indeed. Eastwood actually ran for mayor on a platform to overturn this and other laws he considered too restrictive of business.

The Old Switcheroo

Substituting one child for another is frowned upon in the State of Nevada. That a law like this exists is confusing enough, never mind trying to explain it. As simply put as possible, it's illegal for a caregiver, teacher or other guardian to take care of a child and, when a guardian or relative calls for the child's return, send a substitute child in that child's place.

ADVERTISING

What's She Selling?

Food hawkers need to consider their outfits before setting out to work in Florida. Whether they sell hot dogs or tacos, ice cream or burritos, vendors at food carts need to be dressed in something more than a G-string or thong bikini.

The law is quite specific as to what parts of the anatomy should be covered, including (but not limited to) the person's buns (pun intended). The law notes that inappropriate attire is a traffic impediment and/or hazard.

Dressing up like a giant banana or hot dog seems to be considered appropriate under the law.

Mascot Mayhem

Spotting a dancing Lady Liberty waving from alongside the road around suburban strip malls is as much a sign of spring as the return of the swallows to Capistrano. However, some people find a Lady Liberty, a dancing Mattress Man or a human dressed as a large hot dog more than vaguely surreal—they find them annoying. When those annoyed people get elected to positions of power, they opt to do something about it, particularly in McHenry, Illinois. After all, the mascots could be a distraction to drivers and a nuisance when motorists honk at them.

The McHenry City Council revised a zoning ordinance to ban the use of "moving signs," including live mascots. But what about the person's freedom of speech under the Constitution? City Council argued that these sign-wielding mascots are, in effect, not people but business signs, and as such they can be regulated out of business.

So keep your giant foam mascot out of McHenry. He is not welcome.

Surfboards and Scoreboards, Yes— Billboards, No!

Hawaii treasures the views of mountains, volcanoes and beaches as well as its tourists! For that reason, no billboards are allowed on the island unless they are advertising either an entire building for sale or a notice by the local government.

Three other states also ban billboards: Alaska, Maine and Vermont. Two other states, Rhode Island and Oregon, have prohibited the construction of new billboards.

What Is that Shiny Thing?

Metal foil balloons attract attention. They are shiny, hold helium forever and make any event a little more festive.

The balloons also conduct electricity, and when they get tangled up in power lines, they can cause power outages.

In Los Angeles, you can have a metallic balloon if you keep it lower than five feet (think table-top display). And even at five feet and below, the balloons can't be used for advertising or for promotional or commercial purposes.

Is that Revelry?

When business is slow, using traditional advertising is sometimes not as effective as merchants would like. Which is why some are tempted to break out a trumpet or brass band to drum up business. Advertising such as this must have gotten a little out of control, one imagines, in Indian Wells, California. So much so that lawmakers decided it was a good idea to put a stop to it.

It's declared a nuisance for retailers to use a musical instrument or even sing to people to try to convince them to come in and do some shopping. So put away that tuba and big drum, and stick to flyers!

Going Out of Business?

It's not uncommon to drive by a store that appears to be perpetually "going out of business," only to still be "going" a few months later. It has been reported that merchandise at stores that are going out of business is priced higher than at other stores or even other locations of the same chain.

Some states are cracking down on these type of sales. In Athens, Georgia, stores holding a "going out of business" or fire sale have to apply for a license. In Alaska, Arkansas, Georgia and South Dakota, stores have to be actually going out of business.

Sticky Business

It makes sense that adhering stickers randomly to Seattle Center Campus public property is illegal, but it's also a big no-no to hand out "stickers" to anyone on campus without the director's approval.

Look Up, Look Way Up

It is illegal to tack posters, advertisements, vending machines or anything else on a utility pole in Washington State without prior permission from that utility provider. The concern here is to ensure a safe environment for utility workers. However, should you procure said permission to tack your flyer onto the pole, there's one more stipulation to the process: the poster must be placed 12 feet or higher "above the surface of the ground."

BUSINESS HYGIENE

The Dirt Brigade

While this next old law might sound odd to readers today, it was quite a common statute in the early days of this country's history.

Settlers migrated across the U.S. with great anticipation for a prosperous future, building up new communities as they traveled. False storefront buildings and homes abutted the plankboard sidewalks lining simple dirt roadways. But keeping these new buildings dust and dirt free was a challenge. Shop and homeowners were continuously sweeping the floors of their establishment, often shooting the dirt back out to the muddy front lane.

Of course, maintaining safe roadways was crucial for transportation, commerce building and the overall growth and welfare of the country. And as the main streets of these communities were upgraded, shooting the dirt out the front door of your establishment was no longer an acceptable practice. Hence the reason why communities like Eagle, Idaho, passed a law forbidding people from sweeping the dirt from their homes and businesses into the street.

If you have nothing to do one day and are so inclined, visit your local museum or law library and dig out some of these centuries-old statutes. Chances are you'll find a dusty old rule similar to this one from Eagle in your hometown's history.

Peanut Protocol

Folks in Bremerton, Washington, were at one time forbidden from shucking peanuts on the street. It was likely that the city fathers wanted to keep their burgeoning city litter free. They apparently took a tough stand against town drunks as well. At a city meeting on March 13, 1911, council members unanimously agreed to pass a resolution "prohibiting any one from selling any liquor" to a particular individual whose name was included in the official minutes. Once again, keeping city streets clean was likely a motivating factor.

Ah! He Wet Me!

It can be challenging to position your lawn sprinkler in precisely the right spot. It seems like no matter where you place it, there's an area of the yard that doesn't get soaked. If you're in Helena, Montana, there is an additional challenge: you aren't allowed to wet pedestrians. It's illegal to annoy passersby by sprinkling them with water from your sprinkler.

Silent but Deadly—and Illegal

Before getting into an elevator in Port Arthur, Texas, people may want to take care of business, so to speak. "Obnoxious odors" may not be emitted while in an elevator.

Skeletons in the Office Closet

Many businesses are like people; they have pasts they'd rather not admit to having. In Chicago, any business that wants to enter a contract with the city has to come clean. They have to sift through all their records and divulge any dealings they had with slaves during slavery.

Chicago was the first city to pass what is called a "Slavery Era Disclosure Ordinance." According to the city, the idea is not to bar companies with slavery in its past, but to get information for a possible "reparation lawsuit" in the future.

BOOZE RULES

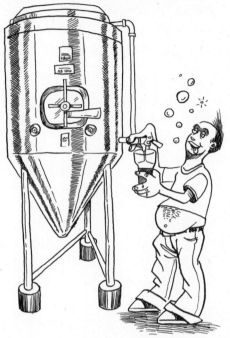

Know the Limits

Two's the limit—two liters, that is. A law amended by Utah's 1991 General Session prohibited licensed premises or any related business from selling beer to the public in "containers larger than two liters." A business can sell containers bigger than that, but they can only be used to "dispense beer on draft for consumption on the beer retailer's licensed premises."

BYOB—Unless You're in Indiana

Thinking of picking up a six-pack and taking it into a restaurant to save some money on the bar tab? Don't do it in Indiana. Bringing your own liquor to a restaurant "or place of public entertainment" is illegal if you plan on drinking it, showing it off, selling it or giving it to someone else so they can drink it.

And it's not just against the law to bring it into these places; it's illegal to partake of any liquor anyone else has brought in (although it's only a Class C misdemeanor). So make sure that toast is being made with restaurant-owned booze, or you could be drinking your booze along with paying a fine.

Last Call?

In Utah, if the governor declares a state of emergency, it is illegal for businesses to sell or supply alcohol to the public. On the other hand, the governor can overturn that law if he or she rules that the emergency isn't serious enough to warrant it. And to muddy the waters further, it's altogether unclear what constitutes an emergency in the first place!

Ship Soda, Not Spirits

Kentucky has stiff penalties for anyone who ships alcohol into the state as a "gift." Beer, wine or spirits sent to a friend could cost the sender five years in jail.

A Tall Cold One

According to a Wikipedia article, beer is considered to be the most "widely consumed alcoholic beverage" and the "third-most popular drink overall, after water and tea." This love of beer, and the pride with which brewers create their product, is centuries old and something the state of Iowa officially recognized as early as 1868. On April 8 of that year, the Twelfth General Assembly of the State of Iowa passed an act for the "Protection of Hop-Growing Interests." Strict regulations surrounded the use, planting, cultivating, transporting or selling of hop roots, plants or cuttings, which is perfectly understandable. However, one can get a little confused with Section 4 of this regulation, which requires the "standard size for all boxes used in picking hops shall be 36 inches long, 18 inches wide, and 23¼ inches deep, inside measure." Hmmm?

Lucky Lager, et al...

Speaking of beer...it appears the city fathers in Bettendorf, Iowa, were at one time quite concerned about giving every beer manufacturer an even playing field when it came to quenching the thirst of its residents. In 1974, the community banned signs advertising particular brands of beer at any "licensee or permittee authorized to sell beer at retail."

Protecting Private Property

Washington residents take their liquids seriously. There are strict laws surrounding who can fill casks, barrels, kegs, bottles or boxes, the particulars surrounding the kind of beverage used and appropriate labeling. Most importantly, it is unlawful for anyone to tackle any of these responsibilities without express permission from the owner or owners of these receptacles. Furthermore, anyone destroying a beer cask, barrel, keg, bottle or box without said permission is guilty of a misdemeanor.

So much as break your buddy's beer bottle, and you could find yourself in violation of this law. A first conviction will cost you a fine of $5 for every "cask, barrel, keg, or box" filled and another 50 cents for every one of these items sold. Fines double on a second and subsequent offense. The moral of the story—keep your hands off your neighbor's beer containers!

Closed Means Closed

Laws around the consumption of alcohol in bars can be pretty intense. But you'd think that if you owned the joint, you'd have more freedoms.

That's not the case in Iowa. No bar owner or employee can drink alcohol after the bar closes. To add insult to injury, tips are illegal in Iowa as well.

It seems likely that neither of these laws is enforced.

Dangerous Saws and Alcohol?

Drunken miners should steer clear of the mine in Wyoming. The same goes for individuals who work in smelters, machine shops and sawmills. The law is stricter when dealing with lumberjacks. Even carrying a six-pack of beer into a logging camp could cost you $500 and land you in jail for a year.

Last Call for Alcohol?

If you're out on the town and cutting loose in Haines, Alaska, you'd better know your limits—or someone will decide your limits for you. It's against the law in that city to serve alcohol to a drunken patron. And when one employee has denied a patron alcohol, it's also illegal to allow another employee to serve that person. In fact, it's against the law for that drunken individual to remain in the licensed premises at all!

It's also a bad idea to allow a drunken bartender to serve drinks. Not only will that get the establishment's owners in trouble with the law, but it could also conceivably carve a few layers off the night's profits!

Junk Is in the Eye of the Sober Beholder

Reduce, reuse and recycle is a great way to decrease the number of items that end up in landfills. Junkyards are part of the reuse section of the cycle. However, in Wyoming, junk dealers are not allowed to buy anything—metals, rubber, rags, paper or other items—from someone who is drunk.

Hope You Aren't Too Thirsty

Many people would say they'd be hard-pressed to beat the pleasures of a ice-cold beer on a hot summer day, but guzzling it is out of the question in Lefors, Texas. Swallowing "more than three gulps" of beer at a time is illegal.

GAMBLING

Bet It's Against the Law!

Gambling has a long and storied history in the U.S. There were
no national restrictions against gambling when the country was
a collection of British colonies. In fact, lotteries were used to raise
money now and again. Some universities and secondary schools
owe their improvements to 18th and 19th century lotteries.
According to historians, the 1769 law restricting lotteries instituted by the British was one of the issues that fueled the call
for independence.

- ☞ Anti-gambling forces in the northeast pushed gambling onto
  boats, particularly in Mississippi.

- ☞ San Francisco was once a huge hub for gambling, and by 1850
  it had overtaken New Orleans as gaming capital of the U.S.

- ☞ In 1931, Nevada legalized most forms of gambling, and while
  most of the country cracked down on gambling, Las Vegas

became the gambling Mecca. For decades it was one of a handful of states that permitted gambling.

☛ New Hampshire broke away from the pack in 1963 by authorizing a state lottery, and other states swiftly followed suit. But now an odd patchwork of laws controls what bets can be placed and which can't.

☛ In New Mexico, casinos on Native American reservations can operate slots and offer all kinds of card games. Strictly prohibited is betting on camel races, ostrich races and bicycle races.

☛ In Alabama, parimutuel betting, in which all bets are placed in a pool and the payoff is calculated by sharing the pool among all winning bets, is allowed. Even though it's most commonly used on horse racing and lotteries, you can't bet at a racetrack or buy a lottery ticket.

☛ In Arkansas you can bet on everything, but Native American casinos and commercial operations are not allowed. The same goes for Texas. West Virginia prohibits only Native American casinos; other commercial casinos are okay.

☛ South Carolina changed its law on gambling in 2000. Video poker machines, which had been legal, are not anymore. The only legal gambling in the state is the state-run lottery.

☛ In Hawaii all bets are off—gambling of any kind is completely illegal.

☛ In Fresno, California, elementary schools can't double-down with poker tournaments or dice games. School funding will have to get a little more creative.

Odds Are Pretty Good on this One

North Carolina lawmakers are very serious about their prohibition on lotteries. Unlike many states across the country that have turned around their thinking on lotteries and use them to fund everything from education to roads, North Carolina wants nothing to do with lotteries. It's illegal to "open, set on foot, carry on, promote, make or draw, publicly or privately, a lottery." This included not just cash but anything of value, including homes, vehicles, jewelry or "chattels."

Not only are lotteries in North Carolina illegal, but it's also illegal to take part in lotteries that take place in other states. The law makes it illegal to even possess a single lottery ticket, even if the ticket is from a legal lottery. Having a ticket in your possession could result in a $2000 fine.

Keeping Bingo Clean

Bingo aficionados tend to collect a great number of good-luck charms. Troll dolls are popular along with rabbits' feet and lucky clovers. Bingo games are often run by church groups and are generally considered innocuous in terms of gambling. But innocuous isn't the same as harmless in Bensalem, Pennsylvania. Lawmakers set one limitation: anyone convicted of a felony is not allowed to operate a bingo game. It's also illegal to advertise prizes in bingo games.

INK INDUSTRY

Painted Ladies Permitted, Finally

The ancient Greeks used tattoos to communicate between spies. In New Zealand, facial tattoos called "moko" mark a person's rank in a community. The tradition of tattooing goes back thousands of years, but that didn't stop lawmakers from slapping a few restrictions on needle use.

At one time considered a mark of criminal behavior, tattoo artists can now enjoy a new level of freedom to ply their trade. In the U.S., tattoos can communicate anything from sporting accomplishments, to devotion to a loved one, to membership in a certain "tribe."

Oklahoma and South Carolina were the last states to consider tattooing illegal. The prohibition may have been focused on concerns regarding the safety and sanitation of the equipment, including needles and ink, although there were also rumored to be "moral" concerns.

That said, many tattoo parlors operated in both states anyway, but they operated in defiance of the law and without the benefit of regulation. Tattoo artists fought citations based on a strict interpretation of the law: since the law stated a tattoo was "a permanent indelible mark" created by a needle that is visible on the skin, attorneys argued that their client's work didn't qualify. Tattoos can now be removed by laser surgery, which means, from a technical standpoint, they are actually "impermanent."

In 2004, South Carolina legalized tattooing, and two years later, Oklahoma gave in to the ink. In 2006 a new law was signed by Oklahoma governor Brad Henry officially permitting tattooing, and it created strict regulations for health and safety that included sterilization of equipment and restrictions on the materials used.

That said, there are plenty of laws limiting tattoos in one way or another.

In Columbus, Georgia, you can get a tattoo, but not on Sunday. Not even if it's a tattoo of a church.

Color Inside the Lines Only

☛ Although tattoos are legal in Connecticut, they are still subject to restrictions—facial tattoos are permitted but may only be done by a licensed physician.

☛ No tattoos within an inch of the eye in Georgia.

☛ Most states outlaw tattooing minors, but if your parents say it's okay, kids (defined as under 18) can go under the inked needle in Colorado, Alaska, Connecticut and Louisiana.

☛ In New Mexico, there is no legislation covering tattooing of humans. However, animal tattooing is regulated by law.

☛ Make sure you are completely and utterly happy with your tattoo selection in North Carolina. In that state you will have to keep your tattoo forever—removing them is illegal.

Pen and Ink

Freedom of expression when it came to body art was under the gun for a time in the town of Brookfield, Wisconsin. An old law in that community prohibited anyone from opening a tattoo parlor or making tattoos unless a licensed health practitioner was doing them for medical reasons. This law was later repealed—no surprises there!

Recreation—
Can't We Just Have Fun?

*Fun is one thing, but all it takes is a few folks
ignoring the standards of good behavior to launch
lawmakers into action. The laws is this section were
made to keep us all playing nicely with one another.*

KICK UP YOUR HEELS

Swing that Partner—Quickly!

Sleep is an important commodity in the community of Devil's Lake, North Dakota. So much so that public dances in that community have to shut down by midnight. In addition, if you decide to host a public dance, you're required to obtain a permit, and the dance can't go on for longer than four hours. Additionally, sponsors or establishments can host only one dance per year, which, depending on the number of sponsors hosting dances in any given year, could mean residents in Devil's Lake have to hang their dancing shoes up for long periods of time.

RUMORED
Keep Still!

It's bad enough that tips are illegal in Iowa, but in New Hampshire the law gets far stricter. Patrons at a tavern, restaurant or café are not allowed to tap their feet, nod their head or in any way keep time with the music. The law might be based on concerns that certain kinds of music is corrupting, particularly musical genres that inspire movement. This would undoubtedly close down all musical venues with head-banging bands.

Dance with Me for Free

During World War II, United Service Organizations had a tradition of operating dance halls, places where GIs could meet up with young women and cut a rug. It's unclear if there was a shortage of willing women or an overabundance of enterprising hall owners, but whatever the reason, lawmakers felt it was necessary to "cut in," so to speak. It's illegal in Washington, DC, to pay a woman to dance with male patrons.

SPORTS

Rules of Golf

Lawmakers in Michigan have put a whole new meaning to the golf phrase "afraid of the dark." In that state, golfers have to call it a night by 1:00 AM, and they can't take a swing on the "dance floor," and that includes putting greens, driving ranges and miniature golf courses, until six bells.

Too Dark to Disc

Some sports lend themselves to nighttime play. Nights are cool, and stadium lights fill the field with enough illumination to see the game. Other games are deemed too dangerous to be played at night. In Helena, Montana, folf is one those games.

Folf, or Frisbee golf, is a popular sport in Montana, and there are a number of folf courses. Unfortunately none of the courses appear to provide adequate lighting in Helena, so folf enthusiasts have to limit their folfing to daylight hours.

Tagging Is Too Dangerous

Technically, this isn't a law, unless you're in elementary school in Attleboro, Massachusetts. The principal at Willett Elementary banned a whole slew of "chase" games during recess, such as tag, for fear that if a child were to get hurt, the school would be held liable. Other games targeted by the area schools include dodge ball (which administrators claimed was "exclusionary and dangerous") and "contact" sports.

Phone tag is still permitted, according to media reports.

Chairlift Courtesies

There is a right way and a wrong way for a skier or snowboarder to use a chairlift. If you don't have sufficient "knowledge or physical ability" to use this equipment safely in Nevada, you are breaking the law as soon as you take a seat. Throwing objects off a chairlift during the ride is also against the law. Skiers below the lifts are undoubtedly thanking their lucky stars for that golden nugget!

Single Ladies—Jump!

There is good news for all the single women in Florida. A popular urban myth is that it's illegal for unmarried women to parachute on Sunday. Like so many of the crazy laws that make their way around the Internet, this is completely and utterly wrong.

In fact, it's illegal for *married* women in Florida to parachute on Sundays.

Good thing we got that cleared up.

According to local skydivers, this law is regularly broken.

Hockey Etiquette

While it might not be an official state law, throwing anything onto the ice at the Joe Louis Arena in Detroit can land you anywhere from eviction from that game to "revocation of his/her season tickets" and even "possible legal prosecution." Tossing objects on the ice isn't all that uncommon, and the first item that comes to mind as a fan reaction at a hockey game is the ball caps thrown onto the ice when a player scores a hat trick.

However, Red Wing fans started a tradition back in 1952 that was a lot less forgiving when it came to possibly damaging the ice surface. On April 15 of that year, a fan tossed an octopus onto the ice—the eight legs of the octopus represented the number of victories necessary to win the Stanley Cup at that time in hockey history. Of course, it became difficult to quickly clean the ice after what, during some games, was a barrage of octopi being tossed out. Any leftover debris could pose a danger to players, so regardless the intent of the flying octopi, they—and anything else one could think of tossing—were banned.

Fight-night Formalities

In order for fighting to be considered a sport in Utah, there are rules to follow. For example, participants must follow a formal set of criteria or techniques. And certain areas of the body are exempt from attack—such as the eyes, Adam's apple, temple and groin. No rushing about, willy-nilly, combining kicking, punching, hair yanking or—heaven forbid—biting allowed. This type of unmanaged, no-holds-barred action is in Utah courts considered ultimate fighting, and it's a Class A misdemeanor to take part in such a "sport" in this state.

Dude! I Can't See!

Many cities have rules against skateboarding, but generally the rules apply every hour of the day. In Akron, Ohio, lawmakers opted for some flexibility. Skateboarding is only prohibited after dark.

Keep it Outside

In Los Angeles, skateboarding and roller-skating are hugely popular. Too popular for the librarians and judges in the county, it would seem. The county found it necessary to add a specific law on the books to prohibit skateboarding and roller-skating *inside* the LA County Superior Court and the Compton Branch of the County Public Library.

It's unclear from our research whether other courts or libraries are more accommodating to wheeled patrons.

ARCADE AND RELATED GAMES

Can I See Some ID?

Protecting minors is a full-time job, even if the establishment is supposed to be for minors. In Nashville, Tennessee, the law is quite clear. A grown-up must be present at all times while the amusement park, video arcade or other fun spot catering to kids is open. And it's not just enough to be present. The adult in charge (18 years or older) must be clearly identified by name, and his or her name should be "publicly displayed" at all times.

Sorry, Kids, No Pinball Wizards Under 18

Louisiana and Connecticut are down right permissive when you compare them to Nashville, Tennessee, at least as far as pinball is concerned. Up until fairly recently, it was against the law in the city for minors to play pinball at all. They couldn't even be within 10 feet of a pinball machine. Individuals who wanted to drop their coins in had to prove they were over 18.

Actually, much broader bans on pinball were not unusual at one point in time. From the early 1940s to the mid-1970s, most of the big cities in our nation banned pinball because those first machines were seen as games of chance, not skill. As such, pinball was considered a form of gambling. There were even raids in New York on pinball machine owners, and the confiscated machines were dumped into the river. Early machines had no flippers; instead, players had to physically bump and tilt the machines.

In a dramatic 1976 courtroom appearance, Roger Sharpe from the Amusement and Music Operators Association proved that pinball had become a game of skill. He played one of two games set up in the courtroom and called out where he was going to hit the ball, and like the famed Babe Ruth, proceeded to deliver on his prediction. Committee members in the courtroom voted to overturn the ban. Later, Sharpe admitted that his pinball shot was "sheer luck."

Today, many limitations on playing pinball remain in place, although no city bans the machines outright. For example, in McHenry, Illinois, there is a law on the books that one must have a license and be of good moral character to play pinball.

The old laws surrounding pinball are still being put to use when they suit communities. As recently as 2010, lawyers in Beacon, New York, used an old law to shut down a retro arcade museum. Apparently, the noise from pinball enthusiasts was so loud that neighbors complained to the city, causing the mayor to toss up his hands and point out that technically, pinball machines are against the law.

Today, only one company still makes pinball machines. It's in the Chicago suburbs where workers assemble several thousand parts mostly by hand.

Mom, Let's Go to the Arcade!

Coin-operated arcades are a concern in other areas of the country as well. In Jefferson Parish, Louisiana, if an arcade has three or more games, like foosball or "flipper type machines," then teenagers need to have an adult with them. It's hard to know if that restriction is more mortifying to parents than to their teenage children.

Dominoes and the Town of a Certain Size

Alabama is very specific when it comes to playing dominoes. Section 34-6-12 specifies that counties with populations between 56,500 and 59,000 must play dominoes in a room with a billiard table.

Doesn't it sound like there once was a little pool hall in a small town that needed some extra domino business, and instead of putting up fliers, they opted to make playing in a specific type of pool hall the law?

Whatever the reason, you may want to check your census numbers before breaking out your domino tiles to make sure you don't run afoul of the rules. Or at least get a billiard table set up in the living room.

Hope You *Love* Ping Pong

There's nothing quite like the sounds and lights of an arcade. The pinball machines and other games can keep teenagers occupied for hours—unless they live in Rocky Hill, Connecticut. Their arcades are limited to "four amusement devices," which includes ping-pong tables and devices that involve "the propulsion of spheres or other projectiles," such as pinball machines, table bowling or shuffleboard tables.

Bed Time!

Tempe, Arizona, still legislates a curfew for its minors. Youth under the age of 16 are not allowed to be "in, about, or upon any places in the city away from the property" where they reside between the hours of 10:00 PM and 5:00 AM. Youth aged 16 and older have a few extra hours before the same rule applies: they must be safely tucked away at home between 12:00 AM and 5:00 AM.

PRANK RESTRICTIONS

What Is that Smell?

Stink bombs have a long and somewhat storied history of disrupting staid occasions. Particularly strong-smelling stink bombs can clear a room or, if properly dispersed, an entire school.

The gas of stink bombs is being explored as a treatment for everything from strokes to chronic arthritis. Research is even underway to put patients who have suffered strokes or who have other serious diseases in "a form of suspended animation" to help them survive the trauma.

Even so, many municipalities have outlawed stink bombs. In Oklahoma City, Oklahoma, no one is allowed to sell or possess a stink bomb in the city limits. Mobile, Alabama, has a similar law, noting that "funk balls" are also outlawed as well as anything that creates "disagreeable odors to the great discomfort of persons coming in contact therewith."

However, in Columbus, Georgia, patience with all practical jokers has ended. Not only are stink bombs illegal, but so are itch powder and sneeze powder.

Clowns might want to avoid the city altogether.

Show that Permit

There is no spontaneous parading allowed in Anchorage, Alaska. No unofficial celebrations and no unauthorized demonstrations are permissible without authorization from the traffic engineer. However, once you've received permission and planned your event in accordance with all the regulations and restrictions as defined, you are good to go. And if anyone disrupts, interferes or otherwise hinders your efforts, that person is in violation of city law.

PLAYGROUNDS

Get Down Before You Break Your Neck!

The admonishments of millions of moms finally has the force of law in Mount Laurel, New Jersey. The city, in Section 107-3, has prohibited all kinds of neck-endangering activities in public parks. This includes climbing on trees; walking, standing or sitting on monuments, planters, fountains, railings, or fences; and for those with creative minds, any property that is not designed for such antics.

So take a seat on a park bench and read a book. That is perfectly safe and legal.

Park Prohibitions

City parks should be a place of safety. Certainly the lawmakers in Minnesota thought so when they outlined this law. According to an ordinance passed in 1999, it is against the law for anyone to use a park to launch or land any kind of aircraft. The law does go on to detail the term "aircraft" to include "hot air balloons, parachutes or hang gliders." However, just in case you're planning to land your little two-seater Cessna 150 in the middle of the picnic area at Charles A. Lindbergh State Park, think again. Not only will you frighten the life out of any resting picnickers, you'll also find yourself in trouble with the authorities. For the folks down in Carver County, shooting off toy rockets in a public park is also against the law.

For Your Eyes Only

Parents strolling through Mount Vernon's parks with their youngsters have more to worry about than making sure their kids don't wander off or skin their knees. They also need to make sure they don't pluck any of the city's flowers. No snipping tree branches to serve as marshmallow skewers and no cutting trees to adorn your living room at Christmas. Flowers and trees, in whole or in part, are to be enjoyed where they grow. Do Not Touch!

Hey Kids! Put Down that Bat!

Public parks are centers of fun and relaxation. But in Canton, Ohio, kids probably want to avoid spur-of-the-moment or pick-up games. The fact is that in order to legally play a game in a public park, there will have to be some planning. A section of the law regarding the playing of games reads: "No person shall play any game in any park of the City except such as the Superintendent of Parks designates and upon such portion of the park as the Superintendent designates."

Slippery When Wet, Goofball!

Cathedral City, California, has a lovely fountain, the "Fountain of Life," that reflects the desert and animals of the area. Covered with sculptures of big horn sheep, lizards, tortoise and fish, it serves as a cool place for the children of the city to bound through—as long as they do it on foot.

It's illegal to ride a bicycle through the Fountain of Life. The law itself is almost apologetic about the prohibition, noting that it's intended to protect all persons using the fountain from getting "foreseeable injuries that are typically associated with biking in wet areas that contain numerous persons."

I Believe I Can Fly!

It's difficult to imagine what went through the minds of lawmakers when they imposed the Superman law in Bromide, Oklahoma. Perhaps Lex Luthor has infiltrated city hall. Or maybe one mother was simply at her wit's end. Whatever the reason, children in Bromide can get in trouble with the authorities if they attempt to jump off the roof of their house while wearing a towel as a cape in order to fly like Superman. Not only are they likely to break some part of their anatomy, but they'll also be breaking the law.

What's in Your Koozie?

Beer and picnics in the park go together like wieners and buns; that is, unless you're in Galveston, Texas. The coastal city, which is known for its casual atmosphere, has one law that is decidedly not casual. In order to drink alcohol in the city park, you'll need permission from the director of parks and recreation. Technically, you can't even carry a six-pack of beer through the park. Section 26-4 with regards to alcoholic beverages reads:

"It shall be unlawful for any person to consume, carry or bring any alcoholic beverage in or upon any park or playground in the city without a written permit from the director of parks and recreation."

There's no indication of how long it takes to get a written permit, but probably long enough for the ice in the cooler to melt.

Watch that Curfew

The city of Mount Vernon, Iowa, is very particular about the use of its softball diamonds. They are to be used for "organized games and tournaments" only, and it's lights out by 10:30 PM, no exceptions allowed. Any other group or organization wanting to use the diamonds for any other reason has to obtain written permission from the city's parks and recreation director.

TAKING A BREAK

No Lollygagging Allowed

It's understandable that law enforcement officials might frown on a person who idly passes the time without intent or purpose, at work or at home. As the old proverb warns, "Idle hands are the devil's workshop." Laze around long enough, and there's no telling what kind of trouble a person could get into. Lawmakers in Minnesota have taken their discontent at this kind of behavior to an official level, naming able-bodied people without "lawful means of support" and who are not seeking meaningful employment as "vagrants." These wayward individuals are guilty of a misdemeanor, according to state law.

In addition, the definition of meaningful employment does not include working as a fortuneteller. If you claim to make your living as a clairvoyant, diviner or any other form of soothsayer, you are placed in the same category as a beggar or imposter and considered nothing more than a vagrant.

Keep Moving Along

Sidewalks in Reno, Nevada's redevelopment district are for walking on only. Sitting or slumbering on public sidewalks is against the law, even if you have your own stool or blanket. This law has been on the books of Reno's Municipal Code since 1995 in an effort to deter the city's homeless population from taking up residence in the area. The law was reviewed, and the area it affected was expanded after a council meeting in November 2010.

You Can't Sit There!

Squatting isn't the only thing Reno's officials frown upon in their city's redevelopment district. Setting up benches on that city's sidewalks is also not allowed. It's against the law to secure a permanent seat "on any street [or] alley" without first getting city council's permission. Imagine that.

Get a Room!

Stopping along the roadside to camp out for the night is against the law in Wisconsin, regardless how tired you are. No tents. No wagons. No trailers allowed on any public roadways or land adjacent to these roadways. Break the law in this state and you'll be slapped with a fine of "up to ten dollars" or up to 30 days in jail. We're not sure of the cost of overnight camping in Wisconsin, but $10 a night seems a small price to pay to set up a tent, even if it is on a rather busy thoroughfare. Thirty days in the local jail, however, seems like a steep price to pay for squatting for a few hours.

CORRUPTING YOUTH

Go Ahead, I Dare Ya

It's almost a right of teenage passage in the U.S. to try to get away with buying beer or cigarettes while still under age. People who traffic in fake IDs do a brisk business among the under-21 set. And many a store clerk has tested nervous teens about the information on "their" driver's license.

Still, many youngsters try to slide one by, and others pressure their friends to make the "buy." The problem has apparently been rampant in Tennessee; it's actually against the law to dare a kid to buy alcohol. According to 39-15-404:

> *It is an offense for a person to persuade, entice,*
> *or send, any child under twenty-one (21) years*
> *of age to any place where whiskey, brandy, rum,*
> *gin, wine, beer, ale, or other intoxicating drink*
> *is sold, to buy or otherwise procure any one (1)*
> *or more of such drinks, in any quantity, for*
> *the use of such child or for that of the person*
> *persuading, enticing, or sending the child, or for*
> *the use of any other person.*

It's also illegal to buy alcohol for children, no matter how desperately they plead.

Swimsuits Require Police Protection

Bathing suits underwent some fashion revolution in 1922, a revolution so dramatic that lawmakers in Kentucky decided bathing suits were likely to cause some sort of threat to public safety. KRS 436.140 set a pretty stiff fine (for the time) between $5 and $25 for people who showed up on a highway or on any city street in a bathing suit without police protection.

The law, which was repealed in 1974, seemed to focus on the streets, where perhaps drivers would become distracted by the number of individuals clad in swimwear. Given the decrease in the amount of fabric used in swimsuits in 1974 as compared to 1922, it seems that the danger to public safety was overcome, perhaps by common sense.

CHRISTMAS

Time to Take Down the Lights!

The holidays can take a great deal out of a person, so it's not surprising that many folks take some time to get around to removing their tree and ornaments. Maine, however, has no patience for serious procrastination. After January 14, citizens will be charged a fine for having their Christmas decorations on the outside of the house still up. Best get Santa back in the attic!

They are a bit more laid back in San Diego. Citizens have until February 2 to remove their lights before a fine of $250 kicks in.

Say It Ain't So, Santa

Few holidays are more venerated than Christmas. Fraught with the controversy that comes up when one mixes capitalism with religion, Christmas can attract any number of questionable advertising tactics.

One tactic in particular has been restricted in Washington, DC. Santa cannot be used to sell beer or any other alcoholic beverage. And don't try to get around the law by using one of Santa's many "Nick" names; the law covers all of those as well.

Other times of the year that can't be used to sell booze in DC include Easter, Holy Week, Mother's Day and other "religious" holidays. Father's Day is notably absent from the list.

INDEPENDENCE DAY

Fire Up the...Sparklers!

Laws around fireworks are complicated and conflicted, to say the least. In Pennsylvania, firework stands can sell fireworks to people who are not citizens of Pennsylvania. Next door in Ohio and West Virginia, those citizens can't buy from their local firework stand either. This means that on the fourth of July, residents of these states have to head across the state border to pick up their firecrackers and sparklers.

On top of that, buyers must sign a note promising to take their fireworks out of the state within 48 hours, presumably without blowing them up.

In Pennsylvania, individuals who have crossed the state line with their legally purchased fireworks can't shoot off anything that has a loud boom or goes airborne, without a permit. That leaves you with the novelty items such as sparklers and paper caps. The law is similar in Ohio.

And while the vendors in any of the three states can sell larger consumer fireworks (with up to 500 grams of explosives) to adults with an out-of-state ID, they can't sell them to citizens of who reside in the state.

However, there's an exception for those Pennsylvanians who have managed to score a fireworks permit from the local township or borough. They can buy anything in the state *and* set it off.

Everybody clear?

HALLOWEEN

Costume Restrictions

What is it about Halloween that attracts so many interesting laws? Is it the masks? The slightly rotten pumpkins? The fascination with candy corn? Whatever the reason, here's a few laws focused on Halloween costumes:

- ☞ Wearing hoods and dark glasses isn't allowed during Halloween in Dublin, Georgia.

- ☞ In Alabama, you can't dress up like a priest on Halloween. The ever-popular pregnant nun costume, though, is just fine. Talk about a double standard!

- ☞ In New York City, if you are over 16, you can't wear a mask outside of a Halloween party. And this isn't just a new "Hey, after 9-11, everything is different" kind of law. The anti-mask law has been in effect since 1845 when some folks dressed up like Native Americans and attacked police. This means you can go out on the street as Superman, but Batman is out of the question unless you're five years old.

Masks at Meetings? Not in North Carolina!

Across the country, laws were passed to try to deal with the problem presented by one of the most violent and infamous hate groups in the U.S.—the Ku Klux Klan. The ghostly robes and peaked hoods became a symbol of racial and religious hatred. As a result, many states, including North Carolina and New York, passed laws to ban the wearing of masks or hoods in public.

This law does effectively ban masked balls in the city. But not everyone agrees it's a worthy sacrifice. Members of the Klan believe their hoods should be protected by the First Amendment. Lawsuits had been filed to try to overturn the prohibition in the early 1990s. However, given the concerns raised by the 9-11 terrorist attacks in the U.S., it's unlikely that lawsuits will be given any credence. The courts have made it clear: symbolic speech has to be viewed in context, and when the context is violence and hate, it's more conduct than speech.

Bright Yellow Guns

From 2002 through to 2010, the Department of Consumer Affairs in New York removed 7500 fake guns from shelves and fined retailers $1.7 million. The law, often cited around Halloween, is in effect all year round and was enacted in 2002. You can't carry a fake gun unless it's brightly colored, and we do mean *brightly* colored. Acceptable colors are white, bright red, bright orange, bright yellow, bright green, bright blue, bright pink and bright purple.

Fake Weapons?

How about other costume accessories? Like swords, billy clubs and nunchucks? Nunchucks, which are two sticks of either metal or wood held together by a chain, have been used in every martial arts movie since the 1950s. They've also injured an untold number of young men in their most private areas. They can do real damage too, which may be why they are outlawed in Arizona, California, Massachusetts and New York. There are Nerf versions if a Halloween costume requires some sort of facsimile. It may be best to go as Gandhi.

Timing for Ghouls and Boys

In Rehoboth Beach, Delaware, you better hit the streets early. All trick-or-treating has to be finished up by 8:00 PM. It's not clear what the penalty is, but it could cost you that chocolate bar in your bag. Also, if Halloween lands on a Sunday, you'll have to move your trick-or-treating to the night before.

Little Ones *Only*

Trick-or-treating is not for the young at heart. It's strictly for the chronologically young in several states. In Virginia, several cities imposed age limits back in the 1970s, and more recently, Belleville, Illinois, has jumped on the trend. The cut-off age for trick-or-treating is 12 years old. "When I was a kid, my father said to me, 'You're too damn big to be going trick-or-treating. You're done,'" Belleville mayor Mark Eckert said. "When that doesn't happen, then that's reason for the city governments to intervene."

Dead and Gone

*The end of life is not without its complications,
but fortunately, many lawmakers have
stepped in to clarify a few things.*

FINAL RESTING SPOTS

Dealing with the Dearly Departed

Here's a law that is a bit disconcerting as to how in the world it even became one. In Wells, Maine, a law specifically states that advertisements may not be placed in cemeteries. Really? What target market is an advertiser going to find in a graveyard? Zombies? The law was recently amended in 2001 to make it clear that operating snowmobiles, minibikes, trail bikes and other all-terrain offroad vehicles were also prohibited in the cemetery.

And just in case someone thought the graveyard would make a lovely location for a second home, the law states that "no building, structure or edifice, except those existing on the effective date of this chapter and those incidental to the operation of the cemetery, shall be erected or placed within 25 feet of any grave site."

We're glad they cleared that up. We're sure developers were itching to open up a new subdivision on top of great, great Aunt

Mildred. Perhaps they'd even offer a special "Garage to Grave" model home.

Deming, New Mexico, has forbidden hunting in their cemetery. Of course, if the zombies attack, we predict a swift repeal of this law.

A Show of Respect

Picketing at a funeral is illegal in the State of South Dakota. It's altogether vague as to why someone might want to picket at a funeral, but the official statute makes rules around picketing quite clear. For an hour before the funeral service is set to begin until an hour after its completion, picketers are supposed to lay down their signs in a show of respect.

Easy on the Finger Sandwiches

There's nothing like a good old-fashioned wake to stir up a person's appetite. Ironically, the vast array of quiches, casseroles and egg-salad sandwiches can rival the spread at a birthday party. As a result, some people in Massachusetts apparently don't show up at a wake to comfort the grieving family; they dive in with great gusto as if they were attending an all-you-can-eat-and-mourn event. Lawmakers were fed up (pun not intended) with the gluttons and passed a law—mourners may not eat more than three sandwiches.

★ ★ ★

Morality Laws, or Blue Laws

All across the U.S. there are morality laws. They tend to focus on what you can do on Sunday, or rather, what you can't, although other days of the week come into play as well. These laws enforce primarily Christian laws around what can be done on the Sabbath, and since their inception, the laws have covered both commercial and recreational activities. While the origin of the reference "blue" is a bit murky, most attribute it to the idea that "blue" was a euphemism for a holier-than-thou kind of attitude. People who followed these laws to the letter were called "bluenoses." These days it's more likely that the affected retailers are "blue."

SACRED SUNDAYS

Closed in Massachusetts

In Massachusetts, General Laws Chapter 136 and Chapter 149 are known as "blue laws." The very first blue laws were enacted in Connecticut by the Puritan colonies in the 17th century.

One example is the state's prohibitions on retailers. Make sure you've bought all the cranberries and eggnog you need in Boston and Bridgeport. Both Massachusetts and Connecticut prohibit retail stores from being open on Thanksgiving and Christmas.

Keeping the Sabbath

Sunday bans for certain activities weren't uncommon in communities across the country, right up to recent history. Even today, many businesses close their doors to the public. And many grandparents can tell of the days when playing cards or going to the neighborhood fair on a Sunday wasn't simply frowned on—it was against the law.

So, mentions of Sunday restrictions making their way around the Internet are no surprise. And the restrictions are only strange if they were still in effect today, when a uniform day of rest is no longer a societal standard. With that in mind, it makes perfect sense that at one time in Idaho's history, riding a merry-go-round on Sunday was against the law. It must have followed, then, that any other fair-going activities on the Sabbath were equally banned.

BRAKES ON CAR SALES

Day-old Cars

Feel like driving around town with that new-car smell on your way to Sunday dinner? Your car will have to be at least one day old—you can't buy a vehicle on Sunday in Illinois or Wisconsin.

Urban Myth? Or Truth?

One of the more persistent urban myths is the one about black cars in Denver, Colorado. If you manage to buy a car on Sunday, you wouldn't have been able to get it home because you'd be in violation of the Sunday "driving a black car ban" in the Mile High City. While we couldn't confirm the existence of the law, we couldn't completely rule it out either.

Pick a Day!

In Texas, auto dealers have a choice: they can be open on Sunday or Saturday, but not both. Not surprisingly, the overwhelming option is Saturday.

ALCOHOL RELATED

Holiday Planning Needed

Oklahoma is not a state for those who haven't planned ahead for their holiday events. The sale of packaged liquor (alcohol you take with you versus the alcohol you drink on the premises in a bar) is prohibited on Memorial Day, Independence Day, Labor Day, Thanksgiving Day and Christmas.

Slow Down for Beer Zone

In many places around the south, drive-through liquor stores are quite common. But they are prohibited in Sulphur, Louisiana. No alcoholic beverages can be sold to someone while they are "occupying" a car. Thirsty folks have to get out of the car and walk in for that six-pack.

Tea, Please

While prohibition of alcohol is, for the most part, a thing of the past, some jurisdictions in the United States are still considered "dry"—they don't allow the sale of alcohol within their boundaries. Very few of those communities are located in Nevada. Nevada law actually requires commissioners within its jurisdiction to *allow* the sale of liquor. The only dry communities are those with laws so old they've been grandfathered.

Now, for a Toast to Victory!

A recent change (2010) in the law in Indiana now allows residents to buy alcohol on election day, making toasting elected officials (and drowning the sorrows of the losing candidates) a little easier. State officials considered it a "moral victory." Other states used to have a similar law, created back when taverns were often doing double duty on election day as polling places. But Indiana was one of the last states to lift the ban.

SHOPPING

Snow-day Sunday

It took a blizzard to change one of the most restrictive blue laws in the country. In 1991, citizens of North Dakota couldn't stock up on Ramen noodles or batteries when one of the biggest blizzards in years hit on a Sunday. Back then, retailers were required by law to be closed all day on Sunday, but after the blizzard, the value of having shopping options every day of the week were more clearly understood, and the law was changed to allow retailers to open at noon.

Off Your Shopping List

South Carolina found it necessary to get very specific about what could be sold on Sunday. It's unclear if state officials felt an overall ban wasn't going to work or if they believed the best approach was a list. Here's a quote that lists the items not allowed to be sold in the state on a Sunday:

> *Clothing and clothing accessories (except those which qualify as swimwear, novelties, souvenirs, hosiery, or undergarments); housewares, china, glassware, and kitchenware; home, business and office furnishings, and appliances; tools, paints, hardware, building supplies, and lumber; jewelry, silverware, watches, clocks, luggage, musical instruments, recorders, recordings, radios, television sets, phonographs, record players or so-called hi-fi or stereo sets, or equipment; sporting goods (except when sold on premises where sporting events and recreational facilities are permitted); yard or piece goods; automobiles, trucks, and trailers.*

Sundays in Maine

Maine was the last state to forbid department stores from opening on Sunday. Maine's auto dealers are still out of luck, though. Fortunately, there is good news for deer and turkeys if they can read a calendar. Every Sunday, they are free to relax because hunting is prohibited.

RECREATION

Hunting Coons

Raccoons must have tipped over a few lawmakers' trashcans in Virginia. All traditional forms of hunting are prohibited on Sunday, but raccoons can be pursued until 2:00 AM. There are two other exceptions: hunting on a licensed hunting preserve, and using a dog to hunt a bear, raccoon or fox. Proof once again that a dog is not only man's best friend but also his ticket to a Sunday hunt. Another alternative is for a hunter to head slightly west. In West Virginia you can hunt on Sunday in 14 out of 55 counties.

Game Days

Until the 1930s, organized sports competitions couldn't be played on Sunday in Pennsylvania. It will come as no surprise that this presented a fairly significant problem for baseball's Philadelphia A's, not to mention dreams for an NFL team. Bert Bell, who would eventually bring in the Philadelphia Eagles, took his case straight to the top. Governor Pinchot worked on a bill in 1933 to pave the way for Sunday football, much to the relief of the league. Not a sports fan? Pennsylvania hunters have some options available. Hunters are allowed to pursue foxes, crows and coyotes on Sunday. Every other game animal has the day off.

Keep Your Horse at Home

Thinking of going a little retro, as in the four-legged drive? Don't bother heading to the horse track in Illinois. Horse racing is not allowed on Sunday unless authorized by local ordinance.

Just Hum

In New Jersey, in 1677, the General Assembly banned the "singing of vain songs or tunes" on Sunday. This law would effectively kill Sunday gigs for most pop bands.

WORK

You Can't Work on Sunday in South Carolina, Except...

You may remember the list of things that can't be sold on Sunday in South Carolina. Well, to put an even finer point on it, South Carolina is noted for the number of exceptions to its "don't work on Sunday" law. After reading through the list, it's hard to imagine who still gets the day off. Here are the folks who can work on Sunday:

☞ People who sell food, ice, soft drinks, cigarettes, tobacco and related products

☞ People who work in radio, television, newspapers and magazines, or the people who sell print media

☞ Anyone who works in a public utility either in operations or sales or in a role that is incidental to either operations or sales

☞ Workers who transport anything or anyone by air, land or water; in addition, anyone who sells or delivers heating, cooling, refrigeration or motor fuels, oils or gases; also included are people who install or sell repair parts of motor vehicles, boats, bicycles, airplanes or heating, cooling or refrigeration systems—even if you clean vehicles, you fall in this exemption

☞ People who provide medical services or supplies, or sell drugs, medicine and hygienic, surgical and other medical supplies

☞ Operators of hotels, restaurants and food catering businesses

☞ Janitors and custodians

☞ Workers in funeral homes and cemeteries

☞ Retailers who sell novelties, souvenirs, paper products, educational supplies, cameras, film, flash bulbs and cubes, batteries, baby supplies, hosiery and undergarments, flowers, plants, seeds and shrubs

☞ People selling their wares at arts-and-crafts fairs, as long as they made the items themselves

☞ Realtors showing noncommercial real property and mobile homes

☞ People who provide any service or product by "means of a mechanical device not requiring the labor of any person"

☞ People involved in the sale or rental of swimming, fishing and boating equipment

☞ All farmers working on farming operations necessary for the preservation of agricultural commodities

Based on this list, the only individuals actually prohibited from working on Sunday are clergy, unless they are selling items at a church arts-and-crafts fair. Children are also prohibited from working in mercantile on Sunday (and what would they sell exactly? bandages?), unless they are conscientious objectors.

Counties in the state can vote to remove themselves altogether from the Sunday prohibitions by referendum.

Grooming? Just Skip It

Citizens in Columbus can't get haircuts on Sundays. At least not from their barbers. Moms can probably still handle the occasional bowl cut.

QUIET!

Silence Is Golden, and the Law, in Little Rock

Little Rock, Arkansas, has a group of blue laws not focused on preserving the sanctity of Sundays but on preserving the peace and quiet of the city by cracking down on "unlawful noise." These laws are still on the books, making the city one of the potentially quietest in the country, at least as a matter of law.

Honking and Parking in Little Rock

A city ordinance in Little Rock also prevents late-night honking at sandwich shops where cold drinks and sandwiches are served. Customers concerned with slow service will have to exit their vehicle and complain in person.

Thinking of throwing a parking lot party? Good luck with that one in Little Rock. Residents can't park or assemble vehicles in front of or around any closed establishment between midnight and 6:00 AM.

Keep it Down, People!

Someone in Little Rock definitely had quite a list of pet peeves that made it into the city's noise ordinances. In addition to the prohibition on honking at sandwich shops, there is a whole list of unlawful noises in the city:

☛ A boiler that blows a steam whistle, unless used to signal the open and close of work

☛ Animals and birds that emit frequent or prolonged noises

☛ Any type of "yelling, hooting or shouting out" near dwellings, hotels and hospitals in a way that causes public annoyance

☛ Vehicles that make rattling and grinding noises

☛ Creating excessive noise near schools, churches or courts while they're in session

☛ Loud noise associated with loading or unloading vehicles, such as the opening of boxes and crates

☛ Making noise near hospitals

☛ Playing phonographs and radios between 10:30 PM and 7:00 AM

☛ Using drums, loudspeakers or other musical devices to create noises that attract a crowd

You can hoot, holler or otherwise make a racket legally, as long as you have a permit. And unavoidable noises, such as those that occur in an emergency, are also okay. But if you've got a noisy third-grade class outside a courtroom and they are unloading drums from a rattling truck with barking dogs at their sides, you may want to contact an attorney.

Drive in, But Don't Get Out of Hand, Folks

The local food drive-in has undergone a bit of a revival as boomers look to relive their youth and share the thrill of eating among a cloud of engine exhaust with their grandchildren. Little Rock has a number of laws to keep the drive-in revival peaceful, including prohibitions on drinking beer; being annoying by "yelling, hooting or shouting out" near dwellings, hotels and hospitals; having a loud or offensive conversation or by threatening or intimidating anyone; and racing your car engine or making weird, loud noises with your car.

Mind Your Manners

Ever read your youngster the riot act? You know—forbid their participation in every bad behavior you can possibly think of, many of which you shouldn't need to mention in the first place? Washington's law addressing disorderly conduct on a city bus is a little like that. It's against the law to litter, blast your radio, carry a flammable substance or smoke while riding the bus. It's also against the law to spit. Anyone found spitting on the bus can be formally charged with a misdemeanor.

Night Owls Should Keep it Quiet

There's a time for everything, and in Athens, Georgia, the time is between 7:00 AM and before 2:45 AM. Dance halls have to wind their "live entertainment" down by 2:45 AM, and it's not just dancing that has to come to a screeching halt. Any form of live entertainment, including literary readings and musical performances, is prohibited within the boundaries of Athens and Clarke Counties between the hours of 2:45 AM and 7:00 AM.

CHURCH TIME

Can You Hiss "Amen"?

In several southern states, a certain religious tradition involves the handling of snakes. It stems from one passage in the Bible:

> *And these signs shall follow them that believe;*
> *In my name shall they cast out devils; they shall*
> *speak with new tongues; They shall take up*
> *serpents; and if they drink any deadly thing, it*
> *shall not hurt them; they shall lay hands on the*
> *sick, and they shall recover.*
>
> *—Mark 16:17–18*

The religious tradition of handling snakes has always been controversial and yet continues from Georgia to Pennsylvania. Practitioners call it "serpent handling," not "snake handling" because of one key distinction: they handle only poisonous snakes, not common ones. Back in 1942, Kentucky lawmakers felt the need to pass a law forbidding the practice:

Any person who displays, handles or uses any kind of reptile in connection with any religious service or gathering shall be fined not less than fifty dollars ($50) nor more than one hundred dollars ($100).

–excerpt from KRS 437.060 (passed 1942, from Ky. Stat. sec. 1267a-1)

Historically, serpent handling was part of the church services in poor and rural areas, but news reports indicate that currently, the services are also held in more urban areas, such as Atlanta, Georgia, or Middlesboro, Kentucky. Clearly, serpent handling being against the law has not lessened its appeal.

Permission Granted

From today's more "enlightened" perspective, where even youth organizations have elected officials overseeing their operations, you might ask yourself why we ever needed this next law in the first place. According to Chapter 36 of the Minnesota Territorial Statutes of 1851, members of any kind of religious society, incorporated or not, were given permission to worship together and, "by a plurality of votes," to elect between three and nine members of their parish to "transact all affairs relative to the temporalities thereof."

Keep it Quiet

Not only can you not whisper in church in Rehoboth Beach, Delaware, you can't even whisper outside of it during services. Needless to say, all rude and indecent behavior is also prohibited inside and within 300 feet of the church.

I Believe

The use of religious tests in the U.S. for elected officials is a sensitive area of law. The United States Constitution makes it clear in Article VI, paragraph 3, that "no religious test shall ever be required" for serving as an elected official.

Of course, it's very common to see individuals running for office attending church services and for controversy to crop up when a candidate's faith is different from that of most of the electorate.

However, given states' rights, eight have fudged the line a bit. In Texas, the law reads that no religious test is required, but officeholders must believe in a "Supreme Being." If that weren't enough, the state constitution requires that the oath of office include the words "so help me God."

These oaths have been historically required across the board for everyone from jurors to state employees, but in 1961, the Supreme Court pointed out it was a violation of the First and Fourteenth Amendment of the Constitution. As recently as 1997, South Carolina's Supreme Court also ruled that requiring an oath to God for employment was unconstitutional.

Irony Alert! Sacred Wine License?

Regulations and subsequent fines regarding the transportation of liquor from one state to another vary, depending on the state. But in Iowa, even a man of the cloth—minister, priest, rabbi of any church, sect, denomination or creed that uses wines in its sacrificial ceremonies or sacraments—requires a license if he's planning to transport his sacramental wine from one state to another.

Amen!

Church services are protected from disturbance in Mississippi. In fact, the entire congregation is in effect deputized. Should any person disturb a church service, private citizens can personally place him or her under arrest.

Getting arrested for disturbing the sermon is no small offense either. The fine can be $500 and up to six months in prison.

The penalty is enough to keep folks awake through Sunday services.

DIVINE INSIGHTS

I See a Law in Your Future

In 1954 in Natchez, Mississippi, the city passed a law banning fortune-telling through astrology, tea-leaf reading and palmistry as well as "any and all other forms or types of fortune-telling." They did, however make a few exceptions. Churches, benevolent societies, schools or charitable benefits "sponsored by bona fide nonprofit organizations recognized by the police jury" can have a fortune-teller.

While fortune-telling by reading palms is against the law, there's no penalty, not even a slap on the wrist.

REPEALED
We think: A Ban on the Supernatural?

Beware you readers of palms, tea leaves, chakras, auras, crystals, numbers or any other metaphysical practice. If you live in Cedar Rapids, Iowa, you might want to update yourself on the rules and regulations behind practicing your craft before you hang your shingle and book clients. That's because several Internet sources suggest that at one time, Cedar Rapids banned anyone from practicing "phrenology, palmistry or clairvoyancy in the city." Our research suggests that while this may have been a law at one time, it must have been repealed since a quick Internet search turned up advertisements for several practitioners of this sort.

Keep Your Fortune-telling in Church or School

North Carolina also bans professional palm reading or fortune-telling. It's a Class 2 misdemeanor unless you're an amateur and are working a church or school function. Then you're safe to peer into the tea leaves and call 'em like you see 'em.

Register that Crystal Ball

Fortune-tellers can find a safe haven in South Carolina, as long as they take the time to get licensed by the state. That's right, in order to tell the future, you need a license.

In St. Louis, fortune-telling is illegal, and so is raising the dead. In the event of zombie attack, St. Louis seems like a good destination.

Still, these laws against fortune-telling are drawing the attention of the courts. One particular crystal ball law was rolled back in 2010 with the U.S. Circuit Court of Appeals decision to strike down such a law in Lincoln, Nebraska, stating:

THE SPIRITS TELL ME YOU CAN SEE THE SPARKLES

If the citizens of Lincoln wish to have their fortunes told, or to believe in palm-reading or phrenology, they are free to do so under our system of government, and to patronize establishments or 'professionals' who purport to be versed in such arts. Government is not free to declare certain beliefs—for example, that someone can see into the future—forbidden. Citizens are at liberty to believe the earth is flat, that magic is real, and that some people are prophets.

Once again, the American Civil Liberties Union (ACLU) has been instrumental in freeing up crystal balls and tarot cards around the country. Just as the ACLU has changed laws on public cursing in Michigan, its work in forcing rewrites of laws of practicing fortune-tellers in Maryland and Michigan, in effect, is reversing their fortunes!

IN THE BOOTH

Can't Decide? Too Bad

Some states have no patience for dillydallying in the voting booth. At least that's the message in Alabama.

In Code Section 17-9-13, it's clear the moment you pull the curtain closed that the clock is running. Voters have four minutes to pick their favorite candidates before a poll worker will approach you to see if you need help. Then voters get another five minutes, and no matter how conflicted they may be, it's time to move it along—unless there is no line of waiting voters. If that voter is the only one there to vote, then he or she can enjoy a leisurely perusal of the available choices.

Can I See Your IQ Card, Please?

Given some of the laws in these pages, it does inspire some wonder as to how some of these elected officials got into a position to pass them in the first place. The answer is in the hand of every voter in the country.

In New Mexico, though, some thought has gone into at least one of the state's voting restrictions. As is the case in most states, convicted felons are not allowed vote in elections. Another group restricted from voting are the insane and "idiots." It's unclear how that particular restriction is enforced, or how one tests for idiocy at the polls. It seems a little unfair that candidates aren't required to meet the same standard, though.

★ ★ ★

Murder and Mayhem

The U.S. is not always a peaceful place. Between the right to bear arms and the ingenuity of weapon designers, there are quite a few ways for individuals to harm one another. Lawmakers try to crack down on the potential for harm, placing restrictions throughout the nation's cadre of laws. Here are a few of the more interesting ones.

GUNS AND AMMO

No Guts, No Glory

In Jersey, there is something a little premeditated about wearing a bullet-proof vest, particularly if you happen to kill someone while you're wearing it under "plain clothes." New Jersey Statue 2C-39-13 states that if a person "uses or wears a body vest while engaged in the commission of or an attempt to commit, or flight after committing or attempting to commit murder, manslaughter, robbery, sexual assault, burglary, kidnapping, criminal escape or assault," the crime is increased from third degree to second degree.

Maybe the outcome would be different if you were in a tuxedo.

Do's and Don'ts of Firearms

There are times when carrying a concealed weapon is in the best interest of public safety. Private investigators, for example, may need a firearm during the course of a workday. Bodyguards might be considered another legitimate candidate to carry. Or perhaps folks simply looking to ensure they and their loved ones are protected might feel safer carrying some kind of weapon.

At the same time, you can't have everyone running around with whatever type of armament they choose. Flashing a machete on your side while riding the city bus will likely cause concern among your fellow passengers. So Michigan's lawmakers have set guidelines about such things, as have legislators in other states. With the proper paperwork, you can certainly carry a sidearm— most of the time. If you live in the Wolverine State, you can't rush into a hospital armed, with or without a license. Financial institutions, churches or other houses of worship, courtrooms, theaters, day cares and sports arenas are also out of bounds.

Of course, anyone wanting a license to carry a concealed weapon must agree to have themselves fingerprinted, which means if any-one commits a crime in any of the above locations using one of these licensed firearms will face the music in due time. The cost of the fingerprinting is free if a licensee agrees to the process at the county office when applying for the permit. Choose to have the procedure done elsewhere and you'll have to cough up another $15.

If firearms aren't your weapon of choice, and you're more comfortable with spraying or tossing something at your attacker, the state is clear about what's acceptable and what isn't:

☛ If a self-defense spray is more to your liking, make sure it doesn't contain more than "35 grams of any combination of orthochlorobenzalmalononitrile and inert ingredients."

☛ Mace or tear gas is definitely out of the question.

☛ And if you're big on daggers, dirks and other double-edged blades, take note: you can't carry any such concealed weapon on your person, in your vehicle or anywhere other than your "home, place of business or on other land possessed by the person."

While it's understandable that the authorities want to curb any unnecessary vigilante behavior, one has to wonder how much damage something like mace or tear gas might do in the long run? Inflammation of the nose, throat and lungs, along with the possibility of a queasy stomach aside, these methods of self-defense are considerably less fatal than switchblades and pistols.

Hiding Something?

It's hard to imagine how you could conceal a weapon six-feet long, but if you could manage to do that in Seattle, Washington, there was allegedly a time you'd be breaking the law.

Old Favorites

Laws about carrying a concealed weapon have been around for a long while, but like most old laws, sometimes the wording used in their compilation was more than a little confusing. Take this 1912 ruling coming out of Pocatello, Idaho. According to one source, the administration at that time passed a law stating that, "The carrying of concealed weapons is forbidden, unless some are exhibited to public view." Considering Idaho was a Wild West frontier, and Pocatello was once a settlement for treasure hunters moving in on the heels of Idaho's gold rush, it's likely that the community saw its fair share of gun slinging.

Although it has been impossible to verify if this is an accurate rendition of this law, it made its way through so many Internet sites we simply had to include the law in this collection!

No Shooting Allowed

A few senior citizens might find it difficult to refrain from breaking this next law, especially if they're bird lovers and an inordinate number of crows and magpies are about. Apparently, if magpies and crows are attracted to your yard, they can dominate an area and make it hard, if not impossible, for other species to build a nest and congregate. Therefore, some of these elderly spitfires may take it upon themselves from time to time to rid their yards of these pesky critters so they can catch a glimpse of a robin or two. How, you might ask, was this accomplished? Why with a slingshot, of course. Pull back. Aim. Fire. And another nasty magpie bites the dust.

Luckily for them, these folks didn't live in Haines, Alaska. Lawmakers there are so serious about keeping their community safe that they've included a long list of "dangerous weapons" in their law restricting the possession of these items. In particular, their "Possession of a Dangerous Weapon" law forbids anyone from making, selling or having in his or her possession items such as sand clubs, metal knuckles or spring blade knives.

Slingshots are also on the restricted list. Stuff one of those puppies in your jacket pocket when taking an evening stroll, and you'll find yourself in deep trouble, even if you are old enough to be someone's great-granddaddy. Not only have you a "dangerous weapon" in your possession, but you've now also "concealed it." If caught, you'll be charged with a gross misdemeanor.

Dy-NO-mite

It's against the law in Utah to build a powder house closer than 300 feet to any residence or county road. In case you need require clarification, the powder house in question is a storage building for dynamite and other explosives in excess of 500 pounds. One would imagine that this law is a great comfort to state residents.

CROWD CONTROL

Don't Throw That!

This law out of Mount Vernon, Iowa, reads a little like a riot act. Residents or visitors are forbidden from throwing, "stones, bricks or missiles of any kind or to shoot arrows, rubber guns, sling-shots, air rifles or other dangerous instruments or toys on or into any street, alley, highway, sidewalk, public way, public ground or public building, without written consent of the Council." That pretty much sums it up, don't you think?

Drama Queens Beware

Utah lawmakers won't tolerate any of their residents causing what they call a "catastrophe." Someone found guilty of this crime includes anyone causing an "explosion, fire, flood, ava-lanche, collapse of a building, release of poison gas, radioactive material, or other harmful or destructive force or substance" and any subsequent "widespread injury or damage."

Anyone convicted of this second-degree felony (for knowingly caus-ing the problem) or Class A misdemeanor (for causing it recklessly) can find themselves paying for the damage for years—they are responsible for covering all expenses incurred by the various authorities in cleaning up the aftermath.

DEADLY DUELING

Oh No, You Did *Not* Just Say *That!*

Many laws are holdouts from the revolutionary war time period where honor meant periodically getting out the pearl-handled handguns. Here is a round-up a laws that dealt with dueling.

Dueling took its toll, but sometimes it wasn't the actual duel that was causing the problems. It was the teasing.

Honor and pride were the cause of numerous duels in the first place, so officials trying to put a stop to the fights felt the need to pass a law protecting the reputation and possibly fragile egos of men who turned down a duel. In West Virginia, it's illegal to taunt someone who refuses to take part in a duel. This includes disparaging remarks in print or writing, specifically "any reproachful or contemptuous language to or concerning another, for not fighting a duel, or for not sending or accepting a challenge." In other words, sticks and stones (and swords) may break one's bones, but insults are actually illegal when you make fun of someone for not accepting a duel. If this law was enforced, it seems likely that it would empty out every high school and most pool halls in North America.

Anyone calling another person out for not dueling is guilty of a misdemeanor and can go to jail for six months or pay a fine of $100.

As recently as April 2007, one dueling law was put to use in West Virginia. State Code 61-2-18 states that "if a person fights a duel and in so doing inflicts a mortal wound, he shall be deemed guilty of murder." The law was invoked when a man helped a woman move, and another man complained about the noise. The situation somehow escalated to the point that the guy helping the woman was shot and killed by the man complaining about the noise. Apparently, this was considered a duel because the man was charged with murder pursuant to this code.

In Rhode Island, it's illegal to even challenge someone to a duel, even if the duel never happens. It's also illegal to accept a duel. The punishment is up to seven years in prison.

In Boston, you can duel to the death, as long as the governor is present and it's a Sunday.

Duel, Governor?

Politics is dirty business, but one must draw the line somewhere. In Kentucky, the line is on the dueling field.

Dueling was a real problem in Kentucky in the 1800s. Henry Clay, who was one of the state's best-known elected officials and was a congressman, took a shot (pun intended) at the presidency and fought in two duels. Known as the "great compromiser," Clay apparently had to fight it out for his honor. Clearly, compromise had its limitations back then because Clay wasn't a lone wolf in dueling circles. There are records of 40 public duels, and it's likely there were many more. Duels were fought over everything from love to a claim that a certain Latin word was being mispronounced.

Someone along the way decided it was time to encourage the state's leaders to set a more peaceful example of leadership. A law was passed in 1849 that no Kentucky citizen can run for governor if they have been involved in a duel. It's even included in the oath of office for every statewide office holder, county officials and even judges. Here's the oath:

> *I do solemnly swear (or affirm, as the case may be) that I will support the Constitution of the United States and the Constitution of this Commonwealth, and be faithful and true to the Commonwealth of Kentucky so long as I continue a citizen thereof, and that I will faithfully execute, to the best of my ability, the office of (OFFICE) according to law; and I do further solemnly swear (or affirm) that since the adoption of the present Constitution, I, being a citizen of this State, have not fought a duel with deadly weapons within this State nor out of it, nor have I sent or accepted a challenge to fight a duel with deadly weapons, nor have I acted as second in carrying a challenge, nor aided or assisted any person thus offending, so help me God.*

Several lawmakers have suggested that reciting this more archaic part of the oath makes the state seem backward: "I've had it at some swearing-in ceremonies that I've been to, they look at you like you're crazy, what are you talking about," said Louisville state representative Darryl Owens. He feels the snickering is a "distraction to a dignified ceremony."

Historians, however, believe that part of the oath is a reflection of the history of the state and should stay. A bill was introduced in 2010 to retire the oath, but Kentucky House Bill 36 died in committee. No duels over the matter are scheduled.

CREATIVE WEAPONRY

Armed and Dangerous

It's remarkable the number of common, everyday items that can be turned into weapons. This isn't limited to fertilizer and alarm clocks. Several states have identified seemingly innocent household trinkets and determined they are actually "deadly weapons."

In Jonesboro, Tennessee, lawmakers who may have recently read up on the biblical story of David and Goliath declared that a slingshot was a deadly weapon. There were no news stories of anyone attempting to commit a crime at "slingshot point" at the time. At last check, slingshots, and the individuals wielding them, were downgraded to mere nuisances.

Then again, in Homer, Illinois, only police officers can "wield" a slingshot. If the law was truly enforced, it seems likely there'd be almost no six-year-old boys left in Homer elementary schools.

The Peace-loving State

Utah residents are forbidden from "intentionally or knowingly" manufacturing any weapons of mass destruction or a "delivery system" for such a weapon. It's possible that one could accidentally create a noxious gas that could be harmful to those who breathe it. However, it's difficult to imagine how it might be possible to unintentionally or unknowingly manufacture "a delivery system for a weapon of mass destruction."

Not So Silly

Silly String has been the life of the party for decades, from the very first moment the "foamable resinous composition" flew out of an aerosol can. It's actually a liquid that, when sprayed into the air, turns it into an airborne string. According to the patent for Silly String, the foamy string lightly adheres to inert surfaces such as walls, windows or the like, but is "readily removed."

Unfortunately, there's some indication that the substance removes a wee bit of automotive paint in the process. This has led several communities to ban Silly String, including Huntington, New York. The town board banned the sale of Silly String within 1500 feet of a parade route.

"We certainly don't want to ban Silly String totally," said the town supervisor, Frank Petrone. He went on to say he was "hoping residents take it upon themselves to use Silly String responsibly."

Silly String is being used in war zones to find trip wires. The only problem is shipping it through the post office—aerosols are deemed too dangerous to ship by air (versus weapons, which are fine, apparently).

Can that Thought!

We've heard of having to show one's identification as proof of age when buying cigarettes, but in Tempe, Arizona, you have to be 18 or older before you can purchase a can of spray paint. If the first thing that comes to your mind is that the authorities were worried the fumes from spray paint might cause health concerns if used incorrectly, think again. The reason for this law is to deter youth from plastering the town with graffiti.

According to the law, spray paint can be considered a "graffiti implement," as can a "paint stick," "broad tip marker" and "epoxy" paint. And parents can be held legally responsible for their youngster's artwork should they provide them with any of these items and they are used for that purpose. There is some question about the reasoning behind such a law. While there is no doubt youth of that age have been found guilty of creating graffiti, it's equally plausible that those so inclined to express themselves in this way can be of any age.

CRIMINAL INTENTS?

"911—What Is Your Emergency?"

Cunning. Sneaky. Underhanded. These are just a few adjectives that one might use to describe criminal behavior. "Honest" is certainly not one of them. However, a law dating back to 1909 in the state of Washington made it mandatory for "a motorist with criminal intentions to stop at the city limits and telephone the chief of police as he is entering town." The City of Burlington's website listed this old but interesting ordinance as one of the strangest in Washington's history.

Anybody Home?

It's against the law to make harassing or obscene telephone calls in the town of Brookfield, Wisconsin. Furthermore, if you allow someone to use your telephone to make such calls, you are also in trouble with the law!

Zoot Suit Ban

Back in the 1930s and 1940s, the city of Los Angeles was dealing with riots between service men and Latino youths over zoot suits. Some people during the rationing times of World War II considered wearing zoot suits, which used a great deal of high-end fabric, unpatriotic and extravagant.

The zoot suit riots, which began in LA, triggered similar attacks between servicemen and Latinos in other cities. Interestingly, Latinos served in the military in great numbers, so the issue may have started out as a way to flaunt the rationing laws, but it grew into a full-fledged race riot across the country.

Still, only Los Angeles County issued a prohibition against wearing zoot suits within the county limits.

RUMORED
Warn Me If You Plan to Mug Me, Please

So much of crime could be prevented if we only knew where it was going to occur. Well, lawmakers in Texas have decided to take the guesswork out of the equation. Criminals must give their victims 24-hour notice, either orally or in writing, of the crime they plan on committing.

Which makes it very important to read all one's mail and check phone messages diligently.

187

Sex and Related Activities

What would a collection of wacky laws be if it didn't have a section on sex? Officials around the country felt there was a need to crack down on all kinds of racy behavior. While times have changed, some laws have stayed the same.

AUTO-MOTIVES

Heads Up, So to Speak

Getting intimate in the front seat of a car is a little safer in Coeur d'Alene, Idaho. Lawmakers passed an ordinance requiring police officers to honk their horns multiple times and wait a couple of minutes before approaching a vehicle where they believe a couple may be making love.

Presumably lawmakers had some empathy for those who found themselves in compromising positions in front of law enforcement.

Because Cup Holders Are Sooo Romantic

New Mexico is known as the "Land of Enchantment." Of course enchantment comes in many forms, especially between couples. And when the moment strikes, you could be at lunch.

Fortunately, New Mexico's lawmakers have placed one minor restriction on the activity. During lunch, citizens are allowed to make love as long as they shut the "curtains" on their vehicle. This "afternoon delight" or "nooner" law has allowed for a very relaxed workforce and, one imagines, a few busy curtain makers.

Ewww

If you're a taxi driver in Massachusetts, you are going to have to restrain yourself during your work shift. It's illegal to make love in the front seat of the taxi until after your shift is over. The law is unclear as to whether the back seat is an option.

Spreading the News

There are some things people would prefer not to share with their neighbors, much less the staff at the local health center. That you are being treated for a sexually transmitted disease is at the top of the list of sensitive information that folks would like to keep private.

However, if you are living in Iowa and find out from your doctor that the itch you can't quite scratch is gonorrhea, you won't have any say in keeping that diagnosis between you and your doctor. A section of that state's public health laws dictate that it is "the duty of every licensed physician, of every superintendent or manager of a hospital dispensary and of every person who gives treatment for a venereal disease to mail to the local board of health of the city, town or township located in the state of Iowa" information about every such case they come across. That law also requires a patient to divulge the "probable origin" of the disease.

RUMORED
Horny?

Cars have long been a locale of sudden fits of passion. Some states regulate the use of vehicles as locations for sexual intercourse, requiring some discretion (see New Mexico's law about curtains on vehicles).

However, in Liberty Corner, New Jersey, there seems to be an acknowledgment that things can get a little tight in the front seat of a car. Making love in the front seat is allowed, as long as participants do not honk the horn.

PUBLIC DISPLAYS

Kissing Up

At one time rumor has it that it was against the law to kiss for more than three minutes in Tulsa, Oklahoma. Really. After three minutes, you were expected to move on to the main event or move along.

Love and the Time of STDs

Love may know no bounds, but Nebraska has determined that there is at least a health-related boundary around the justice of the peace's office. If either person who is interested in matrimony has a venereal disease, then no matter how much they'd like to see past their health issues, the couple cannot be officially married in the state.

It's not clear if all couples who wish to marry have to undergo any testing or merely sign off on a "VD Free" document.

He's Giving You the Eye!

The Big Apple can be a romantic place. The sophisticated bars, the trendy hot spots, the energy of the city; they all combine to make the perfect mood for finding romance.

However, proceed with caution. It's against the law to flirt in New York City.

Men, in particular, are prohibited from turning around on the street and looking "at a woman in that way." The fine for the first flirt is only $25; however, repeat offenders will have to wear a pair of "horse-blinders" when out and about.

There's nothing like a man wearing horse-blinders to turn a woman's head. Turn her head away, that is.

RUMORED
Bad Dog! Sit!

Dogs have a bad reputation for having little control of their libidos. This undoubtedly comes from the propensity for many dogs to attempt intimate relations with inappropriate partners, like the legs of guests.

In Delaware and California, lawmakers decided it was time to crack down on the indiscriminate nature of dogs, at least in public view. It's the law that dogs are not to mate within 1500 feet of a church or tavern, among other places.

There's no indication of who is fined in the event of a violation—the male dog's owner or the female dog's owner.

KEEP IT COVERED

Next Stop, Topless!

In New York, the law notes that if a man can travel somewhere without a shirt, so can a woman. This law also holds true in Austin, Texas.

The women of New York tested the law in the subways. This practice caused some consternation, and after some erroneous arrests, the New York City Transit Authority officially ruled that women can indeed ride the subway topless.

Transit police did note that the practice can lead to "additional scrutiny." According to press reports, the police have made it clear that any topless women who violate the subway's ban on smoking will get busted. Also, going topless as a business endeavor is illegal.

Going topless is also permitted in Colorado. A 52-year-old woman in Boulder tested the law when she began gardening dressed only in a yellow thong. The city was considering amending their anti-nudity law to restrain such gardening in the near buff; however, they later withdrew their proposal. The woman's husband vowed to fight attempts to change the law, and police, who had been called in by area tenants, noted that no law was being broken.

Tube Tops Are Out of the Question

There's topless, then there's sleeveless. And in Maryland, it's illegal to "bare arms," so to speak. Citizens can't be in a public park in a shirt without sleeves.

The fine for violating the sleeveless ban is $10. Interestingly, those who opt to go shirtless altogether (like male joggers) are considered in violation of the law, although it's unclear if anyone is enforcing it at this point.

Does This Outfit Make Me Look Feminine?

Sometimes we search through the closet for the right outfit, but men generally have an easier time with it if only because of their more limited options. But for those with a greater flair for fashion options, Walnut, California, has outlawed straying from the men's clothing department. It's illegal for a man or boy to dress "as a girl or woman" without a sheriff's permit.

There is one exception—cross-dressing is allowed for "amusement, show, or drama."

There's a Reason They Call Them House Shoes

It's the home of the Garment District. the Fashion Institute of Technology. Where the Catwalk Meets Broadway. Fashion is huge in New York, and the city has a few guidelines for residents.

For example, it's illegal to wear your slippers after 10:00 PM. Presumably this means outside of the home.

In the community of Carmel, New York, men must have on a matching jacket and pants before heading outside.

Things are a little looser on the Boardwalk in Ocean City, New York. The only restriction on men is that they must have a shirt on. Going topless for men is prohibited. No word if the prohibition extends to women as well.

And it's still illegal for women to wear "body hugging clothing" in the state.

Is that Razor Burn?

Sometimes you read a law and you think, there's got to be a really great story behind it, but unfortunately when committing law to paper, lawmakers refrain from such elaboration. Still, this is one law that begs further research. In Omaha, Nebraska, a man is not allowed to "run around" with his chest shaved.

Was it a law created by a hairy mayor? Was the razor lobby falling behind in their campaign contributions? The truth is lost to history, but in Omaha if a man is going to strip to the waist, he best be in an unaltered state of chest hair.

For Art's Sake?

Some folks might consider encouraging their children to study classical art in an effort to broaden their minds. But in Oregon, showing children "classical art" that might come in the form of a sculpture or artwork that shows all or parts of a naked body is considered as heinous as if they were exposed to photographs or films depicting "sadomasochistic abuse, sexual conduct or sexual excitement." Oregon law classifies such an action "furnishing obscene materials to minors," a Class A misdemeanor punishable by fines of up to $10,000.

BARE RULES

Take it *All* Off!

Nudity laws run the gamut in this country. In some states, you can only be naked in the presence of your spouse and/or a licensed physician or nurse. Other states have more intense requirements:

☛ Some states are concerned that nudism could be catching. In Arkansas, no one is even allowed to "promote" nudism, even if they are fully clothed while promoting the idea of not being clothed. Nor can anyone rent his or her land, premises or buildings for demonstrating nudism.

☛ Other states focus on licensing. In Kentucky in 1966 two farmers were fined $1000 apiece for violating the Kentucky Nudist Society Act. The Act requires all nudist colonies to pay an annual license fee of $1000, to register all their naked people and to have a 20-foot wall around the colony made of "solid masonry." While the convictions of the farmers were eventually overturned, the law requiring the registration of naked Kentucky citizens is still on the books. Getting a license requires petitioning a local county judge (presumably while dressed) who bases his or her decision largely on the basis of the applicant's "character."

☛ Having scantily clad women around can build business. While we couldn't verify this one, it is rumored to be against the law in Schulter, Oklahoma, for women to gamble while naked, while in lingerie or while wearing a towel.

☛ Precision about nudity can help clarify a few things, so to speak. Satellite Beach, Florida, found it necessary to expand the definition of "nude." The law now defines "nude" as "insufficiently clothed" and notes that liquid latex (whether wet or dried) is not to be considered adequate covering, even though technically it is opaque. There must be a requirement elsewhere in the law to cover one-quarter of a woman's breast, because the law continues to clarify that each "female person" is allowed to determine which fourth of her breast surface area is to be covered, as long as it includes the nipple and areola area.

☛ Apparently "clothing" is a term that needs clarification, at least in Rhode Island. It's illegal in the state to wear clothing that is transparent.

☛ Other states have a much more open view of bare flesh. In Vermont, a citizen can be naked virtually at any time. In 2006, bicyclists in the buff took part in a bike ride through Burlington to protest energy policies. The Attorney General at that time, Bill Sorrell, noted in a local press report that while he couldn't imagine it was much fun to ride a bike in the nude, he said, "You're not gonna end up in jail for simply doing it." There is one place in Vermont where it is illegal to be nude—in city parks. Nude sunbathing there is strictly pro-hibited. You can, however, sunbathe naked everywhere else.

Questionable Conduct?

It's hard to imagine why sleeping naked would have ever been against the law, or how the authorities would know that's how you slept and take the steps to enforce such legislation, but apparently this kind of "lewd" behavior was at one time frowned upon in Minnesota. While it's difficult to dig up proof of the legitimacy of this claim, this little nugget of trivia was one example used by Yvonne Fulbright in a FoxNews.com article published in April 2008.

Another strange mention by the "FOXSexpert" sounds like a wild fishing tale beyond reason or imagination, but since it commanded enough attention to earn a mention by such a notable news agency, it would seem remiss if we didn't include it here. Apparently, it is or was "illegal for men in Minnesota to have intimate sexual relationships with a live fish." It does give a whole new meaning to the term "night crawlers," doesn't it?

Full Moon Prohibited

Unless you're under 10 years old, you are not allowed to flash or moon anyone in the city of Hermosa Beach, California's parks, zoos, beaches, trains, bridle paths, pools or parking areas.

Proving once again that kids have all the fun!

In Case We Weren't Clear

Precision in the law is very important, and a good deal of time is spent on definitions lest anyone get confused. In matters involving the human body, however, you'd think some things don't require tremendous clarification.

In McHenry, Illinois, though, the Municipal Code takes no chances. A 269-word definition for "buttocks" includes such helpful passages as "the area at the rear of the human body (sometimes referred to as the gluteus maximus) which lies between two imaginary straight lines running parallel to the ground when a Person is standing" and "between two imaginary straight lines, one on each side of the body (the "outside lines"), which outside lines are perpendicular to the ground and to the horizontal lines described above and which perpendicular outside lines pass through the outermost point(s) at which each nate meets the outer side of each leg."

It's not clear why such a lengthy definition was needed, but it certainly lays down a gauntlet on how best to describe human anatomy.

BODILY URGES

Hold that Thought

Indiana has a fairly comprehensive public nudity law. Code 35-45-4 covers the usual kinds of things, such as not exposing oneself to others and not engaging in sexual acts in front of others, and while a first offense can result in a year's worth of jail time, the second offense is a felony.

However, the most common offense enforced under the law is the act of urinating. According to Porter Superior Court Judge David Chidester, the most common defense from people who appear in his court is that the need to urinate was urgent, or that the officer only saw the back of the person, and not the family jewels, per se. "The defense of necessity is pretty limited and just having to (urinate) isn't it," noted Chief Deputy Prosecutor Matt Frost.

The bottom line: if you're in Indiana, hold it and get thee to a privy, even if the matter is "urgent."

Thou Shalt Not Mess Around

Generally, adultery is grounds for divorce, but not arrest. However, in West Virginia, adultery and fornication is actually a crime, although it is classified as a misdemeanor. Once convicted, the adulterous party has to pay a fine of at least $20. One presumes that since a misdemeanor is a matter of public record, it could create other, more costly penalties as well.

So Is that Considered Lewd, Honey?

The laws around sex in the U.S. are extensive, to say the least. Lawmakers have focused their sights on keeping order in the bedroom, hotel room and cab. Here are a few examples:

☛ In Florida unmarried couples can cohabitate as long as they don't do so in a lewd or lascivious manner. No "unnatural acts" are permitted, either. West Virginia has a similar law and the penalty can be a year in jail, presumably without their cohabitation partner.

☛ Sexual positions are of great concern in the law. Virginia requires that the lights be off and that couples only have sex in the missionary position. Delaware is okay with the lights on, but also prohibits everything except the missionary position. In Massachusetts, a woman cannot be on top during sex.

☛ Oral sex is out of the question in several states, including Florida, Missouri, Maryland, Oklahoma and both North and South Carolina.

☛ No sex toys are allowed in Georgia or, surprisingly, in Reno, Nevada.

☛ Sex toys are okay in Dallas, Texas, as long as they aren't "realistic." State law in Texas limits the number of dildos anyone can own to six.

☛ Men are to not indicate their arousal in many states, including Indiana and Mississippi.

Location Concerns Abound in Laws on Sex

Don't do the deed in a churchyard in North Carolina. Or in a tollbooth in Harrisburg, Pennsylvania. Or in a bar in Ridgeland, Mississippi. Or while fishing or hunting on your wedding day in Oblong, Illinois. Or in a freezer in Newcastle, Wyoming. (We'd love to hear the story behind that one.)

Sex for Sale

Laws targeting brothels are fairly common. Most states and municipalities attack the problem by limiting the number of women living in a house together. However, there is a certain irony in this approach. In Pennsylvania, it's illegal for more than 16 women to live together, but it's legal for up to 120 men to live together.

RUMORED
Shaking Out Shakespeare

Sex in literature is a problem too. In New Mexico, officials had 400 words cut from *Romeo and Juliet* because they considered them to be "sexually explicit."

Getting from Here to There

Driving can be complicated. If you manage to buy a vehicle (remember, avoid shopping on Sunday in the South!), then there are many, many different laws unique to each state. This section covers a few to keep in mind.

ATTRACTING ATTENTION

Was that "La Cucaracha" or "Dixie"?

Musical or novelty car horns come with many options for drivers looking for a little melody in their automotive expressions. "Auld Lang Syne," "The Calvary Charge" and even "God Bless America" are all musical numbers you can call to life with a simple lean on the horn.

But keep those musical ditties silent in Russell, Kansas. Musical car horns are illegal.

Maybe someone played the "Godfather" outside city hall one time too many.

Slow Down for Fries, But Not Too Slow

There's nothing like a sudden hunger pang to negatively impact your driving skills. If hungry drivers spot a drive-in restaurant, they have to resist the impulse to slam on the brakes in Little Rock, Arkansas. It's illegal to do a lot of things in your car or next to a drive-in eatery in Little Rock, including racing your motor, suddenly starting or stopping your car, blowing your horn when you're parked or doing something that will make someone else honk their horn.

It's also illegal to curse or "cruise," and every restaurant operator has to have a sign that notes these restrictions.

Want fries with that?

Stand Down, Drivers!

Certainly many drivers have entertained a certain dark fantasy during gridlock traffic. Spending hours trapped on the asphalt is enough to drive even the most patient among us a little crazy. Maybe crazy enough to imagine a Mad Max approach to clearing up traffic—ammo.

While it can be somewhat satisfying to envision that rude driver stuck on the side of the road with a smoking radiator, leave it at that. At least, leave it at that in Connecticut, where it's illegal to "discharge a firearm" on the highway.

SAFE ROADWAYS

Holy Thumbtack, Batman!

Super villains can't use their classic car-chase escape tactic on the highways in Tennessee. That's right, throwing tacks on the roadway is actually illegal. In Section 55-8-170 titled "putting glass, nails and other substances on highway prohibited—Penalty," the law reads:

"No person shall throw or deposit upon any highway any glass bottle, glass, nails, tacks, wire, cans or any other substance likely to injure any person, animal or vehicle upon such highway."

And if by chance someone should decide to toss those tacks, that person has to go back and pick them up: "Any person who drops, or permits to be dropped or thrown, upon any highway any destructive or injurious material shall immediately remove the same or cause it to be removed."

Maybe it was a tactic used during prohibition, or maybe someone saw a few too many episodes of *Batman*, but whatever the reason, any violation is a Class C misdemeanor, something that even the Joker wouldn't want on his record.

Clear the Streets

This next law begs the question of why it was necessary to gather all the personal and financial resources required to pass such a law in the first place. But the old saw about "common sense not being particularly common" certainly comes into play. In fact, if some places didn't spell out what "common sense laws" meant, there'd be a lot of lawyers out of work—and fewer laws on the books!

Lawmakers in Anchorage, Alaska, frown on people stringing wire across the highways or dumping glass, tacks or other debris on city streets. Furthermore, if you are removing a vehicle that has been in an accident, it's your responsibility to make sure you've cleaned up "any glass or other injurious substance" littering the roadway.

Move That Truck!

This law was repealed in 2000, but up until then in Cape Coral, Florida, it was actually illegal to park a truck in front of a house you did not own. Presumably if you rented the home or were visiting for a party, your truck had to be parked around the back or a few blocks away at the convenience store.

Roll that Along, Please

Got a barrel? Keep it off the streets of Pensacola, Florida. Depending on what you've got rolling around in there, the fines could be pretty stiff.

Swerve or Pay Up!

If you hit a pedestrian in Sarasota, Florida, the fine is $78. It's a good bit cheaper than hitting a barrel in Pensacola, so plan your next trip accordingly.

Honk If You Love Passing

In Rhode Island, there's a law to make "timely and audible" signals when passing cars on the left. So according to law 31-15-4, a horn is not technically needed. You could, conceivably, shout, sing, howl or hit the siren. Or you could merely honk.

Honking Encouraged

For motorists tooling about on the roads of Ohio, it's a good idea not to worry too much if you hear a horn honking. In the driver's education manual, it states drivers are to honk their horns when passing another vehicle.

RULES OF THE ROAD

Perks of Politics

Ah yes, it's good to be king, or even a member of the state assembly in Georgia. Because when you are a member of the state assembly and when it's in session, you cannot be ticketed for speeding.

Yet Another Reason to Buy that Pickup!

In Marietta, Georgia, you can spit from a truck, but not from a car or a bus. 'Nuff said.

Glad They Clarified This One

It's a little frightening to imagine why this law was deemed necessary. In Quitman, Georgia, it's illegal for vehicles to drive on sidewalks. It's also illegal for chickens to cross the road. But it's probably okay for poultry to hang out on the sidewalks—and a good bit safer for them too, now that there aren't any cars driving there.

Arrive with a BANG!

Driving to Wichita, Kansas? Make sure your gun is loaded. When you get to the intersection of Douglas and Broadway, get out of the car and fire three shotgun rounds into the air. It's not merely an attention getter—it's the law. Maybe the idea was to warn townspeople who weren't used to cars on the roads? Or perhaps there was a need to shoo animals off the streets. Whatever the reason, it seems likely no one is firing off rounds at that intersection these days.

Let Go! Let Go!

Often, it's not the law that is weird, but the fact that a law was even necessary if the first place. This is the case with one law in Albuquerque, New Mexico. A city ordinance makes it clear that it's illegal for cab drivers to pull customers into their cabs.

Most folks would say one of the hardest things about getting around by cab is finding one when you need one. In Albuquerque, apparently the problem is more centered on escaping overly enthusiastic taxi drivers.

No Coasting Allowed

It is against the law in Oregon to coast down a hill with your vehicle in neutral. Vehicles must be in gear, and the clutch engaged, at all times. Motorbike drivers are exempt from this rule—they can coast away.

Hold on Tight!

Moving takes on an entirely new perspective if you reside in a mobile home and you're towing it to the trailer park across town. Secure all your valuables and that kind of move might conceivably save you a bit of packing for sure. But don't think you can curl up on the couch and tag along for the ride—at least you can't in Anchorage, Alaska. It is against the law in that frosty city to "occupy" your house trailer when it's being towed down city streets.

Playing it Safe

In Oregon, it's illegal for minors to travel on the hood, fender, running board or any other external feature of a motor vehicle while it's driving on a highway. One exception to this rule is if the youngster is wearing approved child restraints while participating in a parade or dashing between hunting sites during hunting season.

Slow Down! All the Way!

Hitchhiking is prohibited in most places, but only Glendale, California, has found it necessary to make it illegal to jump into a moving car.

It's possible that jumping *from* a moving car is permitted, but we decided not to test that one.

ANIMALS AND AUTOS

Protecting Your Pets

Tying down your valuables is a good practice while traveling, but as this law points out, it's not always the best option for some more lively possessions. This is especially true if there's a moving vehicle involved.

In Anchorage, Alaska, transporting an animal on the exterior of your vehicle is a definite no-no. No strapping your dog to the car roof in that city, even if you can't find room for him in the car. There are exceptions to the rule, however. Motorists can transport an animal within the box of a truck that has side and tail walls that are a minimum of 46 inches high if that animal is in a cage and is properly tethered or if it's dead.

Mary! Take that Lamb Home!

Show-and-tell can be a great deal of fun at school, but students in Florida should be advised that it's illegal to put livestock on a school bus.

So the old nursery rhyme is true. When Mary's little lamb followed her to school one day, if it rode the bus, it was against the rules.

Count Your Sheep and Your Drovers

Washington, DC, has always been congested with traffic, so keeping the roadways clear is a priority. At one time it seems there was a bit of an issue with inadequate numbers of drovers on bridges. Drovers are individuals who move livestock, usually sheep or cattle, over long distances.

Apparently, sheep are not the single-minded followers as the cliché would lead one to believe. At least six drovers are required in Washington when sheep are being herded over a bridge between

6:00 AM and 10:00 AM, ensuring that at least one-third of the roadway is clear for other traffic.

Slow Down for Old Nelly!

In Indiana, you can't pass a horse on the street. So if you're in a hurry, you may want to avoid all the bridle paths.

And speaking of horses, all cars entering the city limits of Lawrence, Kansas, must sound their horn to warn the horses of their arrival. Pedestrians, you are on your own.

However, if you are in Oxford, Mississippi, do *not* honk your horn. You'll scare the horses.

Four-legged Transportation

Camels may be known to travel long distances with heavy cargo and limited maintenance, but they were not welcome on Nevada's roadways. An old law repealed in 1900 outlawed riding a camel on the highway.

AUTO HYGIENE

Spit and Polish

Some might argue that Minnesotans have expanded their concern for tidiness to the extreme. If you find yourself rolling your vehicle through a few mud puddles in that state, you'd best consider stopping at your local car wash before heading home. That's because it's against the law to drive a vehicle with dirty wheels or tires. Why, you may ask? The answer doesn't target what your car or truck looks like as much as what's on it. It's the "mud, dirt, sticky substances, litter or other material" that your vehicle might deposit while rolling its way through town that lawmakers are concerned about.

He Loves His Car a Little Too Much

Everyone knows someone who ranks their car right up there with the family dog and spouse. They spend hours waxing every surface until the shine is blinding. The tires gleam. The chrome outshines the sun. But auto lovers need to show some restraint in Clinton, Oklahoma. It's illegal to "molest" an automobile.

Car Wash Courtesies

There must have been a time in Detroit's history when car washes attracted the rowdies. Among the typical business protocol of offering good and safe service, car wash owners and operators were expected to "prevent excessive noise and rowdiness" and "maintain peace, order and safety on the premises" at all times.

Clear and Clean

Anyone who has lived in or visited some of the frostier parts of this country might recall seeing a vehicle motoring down city streets with nothing more than a peephole cleared off a frosty window to see through. This is the kind of behavior that sends chills down the spines of police officers in Anchorage, Alaska. Keeping car windows clean is a law in that city.

In addition to drivers improperly removing buildup of ice or frost, the authorities also frown on motorists obstructing their view with clutter—and clutter refers to things or people. Passengers aren't allowed to "ride in such position as to interfere with the driver's view ahead or to the sides" or to "interfere with his control over the vehicle." It's also ill advised to plaster signs or posters on any window of your vehicle, especially the windshield. Naw...who'd of thought?

Coming Clean Isn't Easy

Washing your car at home is a great way to save money, but it's likely to cost you $500 in Downey, California. It's illegal to wash your car in your driveway.

There's actually a good reason for this law—chemicals get washed down the sewer and then drain into the ocean. Residents must wash their vehicles in a professional car-wash facility that recycles the water, keeping it out of the ocean.

CAR ETIQUETTE

Timing Is Everything

Who knew there was a right and wrong way to open a car door? Oregon State Legislature left no room for doubt when they passed their "improper opening or leaving open of vehicle door" bylaw. Leaving the door open "longer than necessary" to load and unload passengers is against the law because it can impede free movement of other vehicles or block the way for pedestrians and bicyclists. No word on how long you can leave the door open when unloading your groceries.

Certainly leaving your vehicle door open "longer than necessary" could cause more serious problems than a fine. Aside from impeding the flow of other vehicles, leaving one's car door open to passing traffic could conceivably result in a missing door.

Urban Legend versus the Real Law

The idea that there is a law against barefoot automobile driving is one of the more persistent urban, wacky law myths. The fact is that no state has a law forbidding barefeet on gas, brake or clutch pedals. So kick off those shoes and drive! But if you switch to a two-wheeled vehicle, things change. In Alabama, you are not permitted to drive a motorcycle while barefoot. No kidding. Or should we say, *skidding*? Ouch! In all other states you can drive a car in your barefeet, but the various departments of motor vehicles across the country note that it's "not recommended."

Right of Way

Drivers in Oregon must yield to any pedestrian "walking on a sidewalk." If by some chance a driver refuses to stop for a pedestrian, he or she can be charged with "failure to yield," a Class B traffic violation. Somehow, we think the pedestrian might have a lot more to worry about than the driver.

Plan Ahead

Youngstown, Ohio, has little tolerance for people who ignore that little needle on the dashboard. It's illegal to run out of gas.

Blink and You'll Miss It

This might come as a huge surprise, but it's against the law in Oregon for drivers to race a vehicle on any state roadway. The term "race" includes taking part in acceleration contests, tests of physical endurance or shooting for a speed record.

Don't Drive Your Water Truck Through the Stop Light

City workers in Harker Heights, Texas, may have pushed the envelop a bit when it came to adhering to traffic laws. Lawmakers felt it necessary to clarify the issue. They passed an ordinance making it clear that public employees had to obey all the traffic laws, period.

DRIVING UNDER INFLUENCES

No Vanity for DWI

Coming up with effective penalties for driving while intoxicated is tough. Some perpetrators don't respond to the usual fines, jail time or having their license revoked. In New Jersey, the authorities hit offenders where it hurts. If you've been convicted of a DWI, then you may never again apply for personalized license plates.

Is This Your Car?

Here's the scenario: the owner of the car is too drunk to drive and hands his keys over to his buddy. However, being impaired, the car owner fails to notice that his buddy is also too drunk to drive. If they are pulled over at Virginia Beach, both can be ticketed with Driving Under the Influence (DUI), even though the owner of the car isn't behind the wheel.

DWI Surfing?

The beauty of a floating on the water can be intoxicating, but in Washington, DC, it's best to leave it at that. The District has a law barring the operation of "any vessel" while under the influence of alcohol, marijuana, hallucinogens or drugs. The law goes further than most, however, by defining "vessels" quite broadly. The law includes "water skis, aquaplane, surfboard or similar device" among the vessels that one should not operate while under the influence.

Cowabunga and keep it clean on the Potomac!

How Long Is Your Arm?

Drunk driving is a serious issue, and many communities have recognized the role of the "designated driver." In one city, though, being a sober driver isn't enough. Lubbock, Texas, has one of the country's strictest laws involving alcohol and driving. It's illegal to drive "within an arm's length of alcohol," including being next to alcohol in someone else's blood stream. This means drivers have to keep their six-pack and drunk buddy in the back seat.

Don't Pick Up that Bottle!

Empty bottles along roadways are an eyesore, but they are potentially dangerous to anyone under 21 in Missouri. The laws are so strict that anyone under 21 holding an empty beer bottle can be charged with illegal possession of alcohol.

No DWI Snow Bunnies

Not only can you not ski while intoxicated in Wyoming, you can't even get to the top of the ski slope on a lift or tramway. Another safety rule includes not fleeing the scene of a ski collision without giving your name and current address to the ski operator.

OTHER ROAD HAZARDS

Parking Problems

Parking can be a huge challenge, and meters are designed to ensure that no one monopolizes a parking spot for too long. There are laws all over the country to stop the practice of "feeding" expired meters:

☞ Fortunately this law allows more room for all the elephants riders looking for a place to pull over in Florida. Elephants can be parked at a parking meter but must pay to park like everyone else. It's unclear what the clean-up rules might be.

☞ Horses, on the other hand, are not to be tied to parking meters in Tarentum, Pennsylvania.

☞ In Marysville, Ohio, dogs can sniff parking meters but have to leave it at that. A canine "marking" a meter is strictly prohibited. It's not clear if other animals, or people, are prohibited from "marking" meters as well.

You Can't Park that Here

Never mind that pickup trucks are some of the most expensive vehicles on the roads, in Coral Gables, Florida, lawmakers prohibited trucks from being parked on city streets or in driveways from 7:00 PM to 7:00 AM. According to press reports, the city planned on issuing tickets to violators and the fines are stiff. The first offense is $100, and if that isn't enough discouragement, the second ticket will cost pickup owners $500.

Don't Poop in the Car!

Cars should not be used for anything other than driving. In the town of Fenwick Island, Delaware, it's illegal to turn your vehicle into a home away from home. Unlawful activities in cars include living, dwelling, cooking, sleeping, changing clothes or using the "toilet."

Dreaming on the Highway?

Feeling a little tired? Tempted to keep driving? Everyone knows it's pretty dangerous to drive when you're sleepy. Driver fatigue is the number one cause of accidents in the U.S. At least one state felt it was necessary to be perfectly clear in this area. In Tennessee, it's illegal to drive while actually asleep.

ALTERNATIVE TRANSPORTATION

Railroad Safety

Train passengers and employees will be happy to know that throwing stones at any part of a moving locomotive is against the law in Wisconsin. It's also against the law to hurl bricks or shoot firearms or any other "missiles" at railroad cars, cabooses or engines.

Plan Ahead for that Trip

There's nothing quite as stressful as packing for a long trip. Travelers have to worry about having enough socks, enough shirts and ample sunscreen. And if folks do forget something, they'll be paying triple for it on the trip. However, travelers are usually assured that the airline is well prepared with fuel, salted peanuts and libations.

Delaware makes no such rash assumptions. It's illegal in that state to pack inadequate amount of supplies of food and drink if flying over any body of water. It's unclear if a few packs of crackers are considered adequate.

A Little About Air Traffic Control

Airplane travel is tightly regulated, even when the airplane is really, really small. In Columbus, Georgia, gas-powered model airplanes are restricted to two general areas. One is on private property, if your neighbor doesn't mind. The other safe fly zone is next to the county morgue.

Presumably the dead, and those who are…working with them, don't mind being buzzed by small airplanes.

Keep Your Hands on those Handlebars

Shouts of "Look, Mom, no hands!" may not be heard very often in New Orleans, Louisiana. Trick-riding on bicycles, which includes riding with only one hand on the handlebars, is illegal in the city. The law also covers tricycle riders.

Don't Skate on the Officer's Desk, Son

Miami has grave concerns about bicyclists and skaters, including skateboarders, in-line skaters and roller skaters. According to Section 70–69 of Ordinance Number 97-3103, it's unlawful for bicyclists and skaters to roll about in city police stations. Also off limits are fire stations.

In Maine, you can't ride your bicycle or skate on any sidewalk. It may be that tricycles are okay, the law isn't clear. Fortunately for all those sidewalk rollers, the fine is only $10.

Destin, Florida, clearly has some concerns with bicycles. According to Ordinance Number 378, bicyclists are not allowed to ride their bicycles inside a cemetery. In addition, bicyclists are not to park their bike right outside the cemetery, lean it against a tree near the cemetery or lay it on the ground outside the cemetery, lest someone trip on it. Perhaps tripping near a cemetery is bad luck?

Destin is also the community that felt it necessary to outlaw vending and peddling at a cemetery or setting up fliers.

Code of Conduct

Public transportation in Michigan is more than dependable, safe and swift. Passengers using railroad trains or interurban cars can expect a pleasant journey free of the lewd and insidious behavior that sometimes accompanies the state of intoxication. That's because in Michigan, it's against the law to ride the rails if you've indulged in libations and are feeling a little tipsy.

RUMORED
Control Your Pickle Juice, Folks

Don't you hate it when you spill pickle juice on something and then you have to live with that smell for the entire day? This must have been a significant issue on the trolleys in Rhode Island because it is illegal to throw pickle juice on a trolley.

It's not clear if other juices are okay or if buses have a similar prohibition. One thing for sure, trolley riders should keep a firm grip on their pickle juice jars.

★ ★ ★

Fire Safety, Sort of

*Everyone knows the legendary Mrs.
O'Leary's cow who burned down a good bit
of Chicago. Perhaps this bovine was in the
mind of lawmakers when they developed a few
of the laws found in this section.*

PLAYING WITH FIRE

When the Rescue Is Worse Than the Fire

Fighting fires can make for some tough decisions. The results of those decisions can end up being pretty explosive.

To be specific, in Charleston, South Carolina, firefighters are allowed to blow up houses. The law was created so the fire department could create a fire break when nearby properties were threatened, a sort of "sacrificing the one to save the many" approach. This practice is not too unusual; for example, in San Francisco, the mayor authorized firefighters to get out the dynamite during a massive blaze in 1906.

Imposters Banned

A lighter has to look like a lighter in the state of Oregon. Bet you didn't know you could purchase lighters that looked like grenades, guns, watches, cars, bullets and many other inanimate objects. You can also purchase lighters that make odd noises or whistles. But unless you shop online, you can't purchase any of these items, which Oregon names "novelty lighters." This law came into effect on June 2, 2009, and is still on the books to this day. The no-novelty lighter bylaw falls under the jurisdiction of the State Fire Marshal, and any fines—which could go as high as $10,000 for persons found guilty of manufacturing or importing such lighters—goes directly to the State Fire Marshal Fund.

At first reading, this bylaw seems beyond reason. A huge invasion of personal privacy, some have argued. Online commentaries have critics asking if there aren't more important issues for Oregon's lawmakers to haggle over. However, there is a legitimate reason for this seemingly strange law. The European Consumer Protection Commission made a decision for its members to follow specific, child-resistant lighter restrictions in May 2006.

The goal was to prevent manufacturers from making lighters that would attract a child's interest.

The U.S. took interest in the initiative, with Maine being the first state to take up the torch for the cause in 2008 after one young boy burned his eye playing with this kind of lighter. Oregon is one of at least 20 states in the U.S. banning novelty lighters. Other states include, in alphabetical order: Alabama, Alaska, Arizona, California, Connecticut, Illinois, Iowa, Kentucky, Maryland, Michigan, Missouri, New Jersey, New York, Ohio, Texas, Vermont, Virginia and Washington.

A Safe Kids USA report citing statistics from 2008 indicate that about 53,000 "fires reported to U.S. fire departments were started by children playing, often with matches and lighters." Reflecting on that kind of statistic, it looks like banning novelty lighters isn't such a strange law after all.

Douse that Torch

A burning torch might have lit the way for midnight travelers in the past, but carrying one in Wisconsin these days goes against state law. Since 1977, waving around a burning torch in this state is considered the negligent handling of burning materials that could, potentially, put people or property at risk and result in a Class A misdemeanor.

Fire Restrictions

Another fire-related faux pas in the State of Wisconsin is when a person sets his or her own building ablaze "under circumstances in which he or she should realize he or she is creating an unreasonable risk of death or great bodily harm to another or serious damage to another's property." You can't torch your friend's house under these "circumstances" either. There is no mention that any law is broken if the dwelling is torched "safely."

Tourism and Travel

Going to new places can be exciting—and subject to restrictions. There are laws on the books limiting the time you can take to capture the perfect picture to the correct pronunciation of certain town names. Before packing for a new destination, it might be a good idea to keep some of the laws in this section in mind!

HOTEL RULES

There's Nothing Worse Than Cold Toes

When you are governor, you can insist on many things. The infamous Ma Ferguson, the first female governor in the U.S., refused to let anyone smoke in the Texas governor's mansion. She also prohibited foul language. Those demands seem pretty reasonable when compared to Oklahoma governor Alfalfa Bill Murray's. In 1908, Murray, who was quite tall, passed a law that required all hotels to have sheets that covered the bed with three feet of linen to spare. It was called the "nine foot sheet" law and was on the books for several decades.

So Are You an Extra Large?

It's one thing to require all the sheets to be long enough, but a whole other thing to actually clothe your guests. That's the law in Hastings, Nebraska. Every hotel owner has to provide guests with "a clean and pressed nightshirt."

The lawmakers in Hastings were quite concerned that couples would sleep in the nude, so they made that illegal in hotels, even for married people. And with the hotel owner providing the nightshirts, there is no excuse now, is there?

The topper is that couples are not allowed to engage in intercourse while wearing the pressed nightshirt. It certainly made for quiet nights in hotels in Hastings.

Mr. and Mrs. Smith Slept Here

It's against the law to sign in as someone other than yourself at an inn in New Hampshire, bring in fake luggage, use a fake or canceled credit card, skulk away with aforementioned fake luggage or in any other way attempt to evade paying for a good night's sleep.

Rug Burns Not Permitted

Back in the 1950s, the *I Love Lucy* show was famous for its twin beds in Ricky and Lucy's bedroom. Somewhere along the way, legislators in North Carolina felt that two double beds were the way to go in all hotels in the state. They went so far as to include hotels renting rooms to couples—the rooms had to have two double beds and a distance requirement between the beds of two feet.

Perhaps someone was concerned about what could happen in the small space, so the law was written prohibiting people from making love on the floor between the beds. It's unclear who would be enforcing this particular provision.

Are You Sure It's New?

When is an item new, from a technical standpoint? It would seem to be quite clear; however, in Detroit, lawmakers felt it was necessary to clarify the point. They passed a law defining what it was that made a set of bedding "new." Basically something was new if it was made of new material and was labeled as such. This seems a bit obvious, but it's probably best not to imagine what inspired this bit of lawmaking.

HOW TO BE A GOOD TOURIST

Are You from Out of Town?

Many cities across the country have odd-sounding names, or names that require residency to pronounce correctly. But only one city was so fed up with mispronunciations of its name that officials have made it against the law. In Joliet, Illinois, it is illegal to say "Jolly–ette" instead of the proper "Joe–lee–ette" and is punishable by a $5 fine.

Yes, It's Beautiful, Now Move!

The nation's capital has some of the most stunning monuments and public spaces in the country. There are dozens of monuments, memorials and museums scattered throughout Washington, DC. As such, in front of each attraction are dozens of tourists taking photos. This phenomenon can be a bit aggravating to those who work in the District and get a bit irritated at the delay these shutterbugs can cause by trying to make sure that all 40 people in their group shot have their eyes open for the photo. The problem can get worse with professional photographers who have been hired to capture the journey of various dignitaries and diplomats.

There is a law to limit the amount of time a photographer can "impede traffic" on a street, sidewalk or other public space. After five minutes, it's time to move on.

IT'S NOT ALL EASY IN THE HOME OF THE BIG EASY

Is It Noise or Music?

The tradition of street musicians is pretty strong in Louisiana. In fact, as far back as 1833, newspapers in New Orleans noted at least 10 different brass bands, known locally as "companies," ready to march. They started out primarily as military bands, but it only took a bit of good weather to get them on the street, adding some pomp to any occasion.

But someone else was out there blowing horns—carriage drivers. Their sound was more akin to a screech and may be the reason the city felt the need to quiet things down. In 1856, the officials passed the city's first "noise" ordinance, which prohibited beating a drum, blowing a horn or sounding a trumpet "in any street or public place within the limits of the city"—except when done by military bands and processions. At that point in the city's history, a giant loophole was created that did a great deal to create the brass street band tradition of New Orleans.

Of course, simply because the city is nicknamed the "Big Easy" doesn't mean it was easygoing from then on out.

The next fight came in 1917 when the city council adopted a resolution requiring the owners of restaurants and barrooms to obtain "mayoral permission before presenting musical entertainment." According to the New Orleans musicians newspaper *Off-Beat*, "the targets of the law were the so-called cabarets, loosely defined by Superintendent Mooney as establishments combining music, dancing and 'women of questionable character.'" Unsurprisingly, the mayor's dear friend developed a near monopoly on musical cabarets.

Most recently, New Orleans has begun enforcing a curfew of 8:00 PM on street musicians. Residents seem to largely side with the musicians that the curfew is a little early, but as of 2012, the curfew remains in place. In fact, many musicians have pointed out that the law, if enforced to the letter, would forbid whistling or strumming a guitar by the lake for half the day.

Down the road in Lafayette, it's illegal to play a musical instrument in order to attract attention—unless you have a license. However, if the musician is merely playing for *joi de vivre*, it's presumably legal!

A Toast to this Meeting!

Few places have a reputation for knowing how to have a good time quite like New Orleans, Louisiana. Land of the Big Easy and Mardi Gras, New Orleans is where the Hurricanes come in a glass and can knock the mighty off their bar stools.

Indeed, alcohol consumption seems to go hand-in-hand with many activities in the city, and at one point, perhaps one activity too many.

Lawmakers have to do many difficult things, one of which was so tough it was driving them to drink: attend public meetings. The goal of the prohibition may have been to ensure no crazy laws got passed while city commissioners were "under the influence." But it wasn't enough to stop the elected officials. If they couldn't have fun, no one was going to.

The law, as passed, prohibited drinking during public meetings altogether. Specifically, "councilmembers, board or commission members, directors, and employees of the city, or any other person," are not allowed to consume "alcoholic beverages in the council chamber or any other public meeting room or facility owned, rented or leased by the city during any public meeting."

The fine could be up to $50; however, the law was written to escalate the punishment, perhaps predicting that some would find a good hard drink worth a $50 fine. For those who elect to keep the booze flowing at the meetings, the fines rise, and by the hird conviction, the offender could be fined up to $300 and spend 10 days in jail.

Mardi Gras Parade Rules

Mardi Gras is one of the biggest, most raucous festivals in the United States, and the parade has a reputation of being very racy. So it seems a little surprising that there are many rules about what can and can't be done in the parade route, mostly focused on what can't be thrown during the parade.

It's common for parade participants to throw Mardi Gras beads to the crowd. It is, however, illegal to throw beads from a third-story window. Other prohibited "throws":

☛ Any noxious substance or any liquid intended to be poured, tossed, handed out or otherwise distributed

☛ Any insects, marine life, rodents, fowl or other animals, dead or alive

☛ "Silly string" or other such item which, when used, emits an adhesive string-like or adhesive streamer-like substance that is shot or expelled from a pressurized container

☛ No boxes including corrugated boxes

☛ No condoms

Anyone who tosses prohibited items will be tossed from the parade, ironically.

Keep Your Candy, Mr. News Anchor

During the Mardi Gras parade, there is plenty of tossing of goodies. Approved items to throw include Mardi Gras beads and candy. However, what is thrown is not the only part of what is regulated in the parade. The "tossers" are also restricted. For example, members of marching bands as well as news reporters are not allowed to "toss, hand out or otherwise distribute doubloons, trinkets, or other throws."

Approved tossers are float riders who are members or special guest celebrities of the carnival organization.

Keep Away from Open Flames

Mardi Gras parades in New Orleans could be diplomatically described as sexually suggestive. However, there is one vice that is not allowed on a parade float. Smoking. Not only is smoking prohibited, but every float must also have a sign affixed to it that states the float is a no-smoking zone.

This may have come about because of the extremely flammable nature of most float decoration materials. Or there could be concerns about second-hand smoke for the revelers. Whatever the reason, the air is noticeably clear above the parade route.

Parade Viewing

It can be tough to get a good view of the festivities during the parades of Mardi Gras, which has led to some parade goers to try to rise above it all. They've done so using ladders chained to light poles, utility poles and other public property. These days, the practice is strictly prohibited; however, ladders that are not chained to anything are fine, as long as they are structurally sound.

The Snake Ban

Pretty much anything goes in the Mardi Gras parade. Anything but snakes.

Snakes are banned from coming within 200 feet of the parade route for two hours before the parade starts and one hour after it's over.

According to news reports, the law was passed because people were wearing their pet snakes as scarves, making other revelers somewhat uncomfortable. And, as the Louisiana Purchase Gardens & Zoo direct observed, when you wear a snake like that, "a whole lot can go wrong."

It's Better (and Legal) to Receive, But Not Give

Mardi Gras parade watchers often come away with loads of trinkets from the parade, but it's best not to respond in kind. It's against the law to toss anything to parade participants, including cold drinks, food or snakes.

The law doesn't specify snakes, but it stands to reason given the prohibition of having snakes within 200 feet of the parade.

Miscellaneous

Some laws not only defy logic, but they also defy categorization. This section contains a collection of some crazy laws and ordinances.

TECHNOLOGY

Lights Out

Bright lights can be a crime deterrent, but they can also be a sleep deterrent. In University City, Missouri, it's illegal to have lights in a house that will shine directly into the window of a neighboring house.

Recycle that Radio

Don't even consider flattening your old and damaged radio. Even if the thing is completely dead, there was a time when destroying your radio in Detroit was against the law. It appears recycling has been the way to go for some time in the Renaissance City!

It's a Rolex! Really!

Sometimes a law is funny only because we've forgotten what some of the words mean. In McKeesport, Pennsylvania, for example, "watch stuffers" are illegal. Watch stuffers were often outlawed around the country right along with pickpockets, confidence men and thieves. A watch stuffer's specialty was selling fake gold watches and jewelry to naïve citizens.

Don't Point!

Utah has a law outlining the "unlawful use of a laser pointer." It's illegal in that state to direct "a beam of laser light from a laser pointer" at certain people or in certain situations. For example, you can't flash your light into an oncoming motor vehicle. It's also against the law to flash the light at a police officer— although one would wonder what might ever possess anyone to do that and think they wouldn't get into trouble for it?

HISTORY AND LEGEND

Bigfoot Haven

Skamania County, Washington, has a special provision for the ape-like creature routinely called Bigfoot or Sasquatch. Several reported sightings of this illusive entity in that area and ongoing research that supports the possibility the creature does actually exist prompted lawmakers to pass the "Undiscovered Species Protection Act" back in 1969. The law states that any "premeditated, willful and wanton slaying, harassing or any malicious activities upon such creature" is not merely a misdemeanor; it is considered a felony. Anyone found guilty of this crime can face a fine of up to $100,000, a term of 10 years in jail or a combination of the two. Any fines collected in connection with this crime would be "donated to a state college for future studies and or the protection of said creatures." Strange law though it may be, ignorance of its existence will not be considered a defense.

In 1992, Whatcom, Washington, also declared their county a "Sasquatch Protection and Refuge Area."

Keys to the City's History

In Detroit, the job of collecting, storing and managing the city's historical books, photographs, papers and related documents is designated to the city historiographer. It's a huge responsibility, one that's assigned by the city council. It's also a labor of love, it appears, since the position is an honorary one with "no compensation…allowed."

Sale or Rent?

This is another one of those laws that may leave you scratching your head and wondering why it was necessary to pen it. Arizona's "Fair Housing" law makes it illegal to refuse to sell or rent a property to someone based on their "race, color, religion, sex, national origin, [and] familial status…or handicap."

Happy Francis Willard Day!

Every state has its hometown hero, and a few states are bound and determined to make sure those heroes are never forgotten. In South Carolina, Francis Willard is that hero.

Willard was the national president of the World Woman's Christian Temperance Union (the World WCTU) in 1879. She was a woman ahead of her time from a marketing standpoint when she developed the slogan "Do Everything."

In her case she was encouraging the women of WCTU to do everything from lobbying to preaching to education, and she originally focused on the "evils of intemperance." Willard eventually moved on to social justice issues, which were as varied as federal aid to education, free school lunches, the eight-hour workday, strong anti-rape laws and protections against child abuse.

Given Willard's accomplishments, the state legislature mandates that all schools must prepare a "suitable program" for Francis Willard Day, which is celebrated on the fourth Friday in October. Specifically, children are to be taught the "evils of intemperance."

NO DISGUISES

Keeping it Real

Nothing is more distracting in church than hearing laughter. Of course, you could argue that it would help make some sermons go a little faster. Some parishioners in Alabama may have taken it upon themselves to generate a few chuckles. However, it's illegal to wear a fake mustache in church—if it causes laughter.

There is an online petition calling for the repeal of the law, noting that some people may lack "facial hair and they might want to use a fake mustache to feel more masculine." Allowing churches in Alabama to keep the ban in place is "outcasting of the un-hairy," according to the petition sponsor.

The petition has only a few thousand signatures, so it appears the ban will continue. However, the restriction doesn't apply to fake beards, so men who feel the need to lighten the mood in church are free to grow facial hair below the bottom lip.

Have You Been Here Before?

Along the same lines as the fake mustache law, it's illegal in Texas to show up in church wearing a disguise. Rather than cracking down on jokers in church, it's likely this law was focused on having an effect on the Ku Klux Klan, which had often couched its activities as religion based.

THIS AND THAT

Anyone Got a Broom?

Periodically, fundraising event organizers will send out an invitation filled with bits of confetti, causing quite a mess when the unsuspecting recipient opens the envelope. Confetti-filled eggs are also a tradition during "Fiesta," a huge public celebration in San Antonio, Texas.

But Mobile, Alabama, has no tolerance for those tiny pieces of colorful paper. According to Section 39-77, it is illegal to "have in possession, keep, store, use, manufacture, sell, offer for sale, give away or handle any confetti" or its equivalent.

Perhaps someone sent the wrong person one too many confetti-filled envelopes?

Odd or Even?

The city of Cottage Grove, Minnesota, plays the odd-and-even game when it comes to watering their lawns. That city instituted an odd-even watering law some years back. Simply put, people with even-numbered houses watered their lawns and gardens on even-numbered days and odd-numbered homes watered on odd-numbered days. If a month has 31 days, that day is a free-for-all, meaning everyone can water their lawns!

The law, which is in place in many cities throughout the country during drought conditions, is in effect year round in Cottage Grove. Makes it easier to know when to set out the sprinklers!

Mind Your Ps and Qs

Delinquent juvenile girls in and around Grand Mound, Washington, have been afforded specialized training at the Maple Lane School since 1914. To ensure growth and discipline, officials at the school were strict about who was and wasn't allowed on site. In fact, anyone venturing on to school property without explicit consent of the superintendent was guilty of intrusion or interference and could be charged with a misdemeanor.

The Real Deal

It is against the law in Arizona to manufacture a fake drug and pass it off as the real deal. That rule applies to prescription and over-the-counter drugs, which is comforting to know since we rely on these medicines to recover from illness.

It is strange, though, to learn that this law also applies to the manufacture of dangerous and narcotic drugs like methamphetamine and cocaine. No fake powdery stuff can be passed around the streets of this state. And if you're caught trying to pass off a fake drug of any kind as a real one, you cannot claim ignorance to its counterfeit nature. Knowingly or unknowingly, if you're found guilty of breaking this law, you will be slammed with a Class 5 felony.

Pot Penalties

If you're pulled over in Oregon and found with an ounce or more of marijuana in your possession, you are guilty of breaking the law. If, however, you have a few grams less than an ounce on your person, you aren't likely to suffer as many, if any, consequences— it amounts to a lot of red tape and taxpayers money for what some could argue was for personal use and not to sell. If, on the other hand, you use marijuana for a medical condition, you need a state-issued permit and a doctor's prescription. Even with these medical-related documents, you can only smoke marijuana on your own property.

★ ★ ★

Fact or Fiction?

A whole host of laws make the rounds on the Internet, but it's unclear if they have ever really been the law. This section covers a few of the more popular "laws."

DESERT DWELLERS

Is That a Camel? Don't Shoot!

One of the most persistent, wacky law stories comes from Arizona. In 1856–57, the U.S. Army decided they needed to experiment with some different transportation options for sandy conditions. They imported herds of camels, forming a short-lived Camel Corp to move freight in the desert. It's not clear why this practice was abandoned; after all, camels are well suited to the task, although perhaps not as disciplined as the army requires. Then there's the whole spitting thing.

Whatever the reason, the army sold their surplus camels, but somewhere along the way, a story started that it was actually illegal to hunt camels in Arizona. Given that most of the camels in Arizona now are in the hands of private groups such as zoos and circuses, this story is probably effectively true, even if there isn't a law singling out the dromedaries.

Thirsty? Just Speak Up!

Speaking of camels, not many creatures in Arizona can go days without water, especially when temperatures can reach 120°F in the summer. So it's not surprising that there's been quite a bit of controversy over whether there's a law against not providing water to a thirsty person. According to the urban legends, several convenience stores have been fined for not providing water to people who have asked for it—presumably for free.

The idea of having such a law probably comes from the persistent image in cartoons of a man crawling through the desert, coming upon a store, only to find out that it doesn't accept credit cards.

While an argument can be made that failing to give a thirsty person water is a violation of the more general "render aid" kind of law, it's not clear if you can be fined for turning away someone who would just like to wet their whistle. Even if it's hot enough to boil water outside.

FASHION RELATED

Take a Minute and Get Dressed

There's a rumored law in California that prohibits women from driving in their housecoats.

Show Your Legs, Ladies

Another persistent wacky law myth is the law prohibiting women in Tucson from wearing pants. It's unclear where this particular law myth came from, but its origins are probably from a law more than 100 years old. Back then, the law stated that an individual was prohibited from appearing in public in clothing that was not of his or her sex.

Note the law says his "or" her. Presumably this could mean that men couldn't wear skirts or ruffled blouses. If the law is still on the books, it has not been enforced, particularly on the golf courses of Arizona where pants are worn that certainly cross the line.

Wear it Long

School teachers have it rough. There are all the tests, rules for interacting with parents, noisy and disruptive classes, constant changes in curriculum and the dreaded bob rule. In Arkansas, schoolteachers who bob their hair cannot get a raise.

Where's that Cow?

There's an old insult in the West when referring to someone as a poser: "He's all hat and no cattle." Well, in Blythe, California, the saying must have been "He's all boots and no cattle." Rumor has it that it was against the law to wear cowboy boots unless a person owned at least two cows.

SOON TO BE REPEALED
Is that Her Underwear?

Challenges are underway to repeal many laws—tattooing recently became legit in the last holdout state, South Carolina. Here's one law that is bound to hit the "outta here" category.

Clothesline bans are in effect in thousands of communities across the country. A few have opted for a halfway approach to the issue. In Columbia, Maryland, clotheslines are banned, but you can toss your clothes over a fence. This is also the city that also allows you to have a 25-foot-tall satellite dish but not an antenna. But we digress.

Petitions and protests are underway throughout the U.S. calling for a repeal of clothesline bans. After all, clotheslines are a great way to reduce the nation's huge carbon footprint since dryers use up to 10 percent of a home's energy consumption. But homeowner associations are appalled. Noting that it's hard enough to sell a house, they claim seeing undies flapping in the breeze drives down property values in a neighborhood as much as 15 percent.

ALMOST A LAW

Nixing Saint Nicholas

Albuquerque, New Mexico, certainly doesn't gain many brownie points among children as a great place to live. That's because, as several Internet sources suggest, a council member in that community sought to introduce a ban on Santa Claus. The motion was allegedly defeated. And while we couldn't find any documents supporting this claim, actions to ban various customs or celebrations with religious affiliations certainly aren't uncommon occurrences.

In June 2012, an Internet-based news, information and opinion site called The Blaze wrote about how a group of atheists pushed for, and succeeded in acquiring, a ban on "nativity and religious scenes" at Palisades Park in Santa Monica, California.

And in December 2011, FOX News ran a story about a battle between a Massachusetts school system and the firefighters in that community. Since 1960, children in Saugus, Massachusetts, have been treated to a visit from the jolly gent via the efforts of that community's firefighters who visited each classroom every Christmas. The school system wanted to ban the tradition, arguing its religious affiliation. The firefighters argued that Santa was not a "religious figure—and is not mentioned anywhere in the biblical story of the birth of Jesus." In response to the council's ban on the tradition, the North Shore Tea Party held a "Stop the Santa Claus Ban" rally supporting the Saugus firefighters. No word on the result as of the writing of this book. Clearly, the Grinch is alive and well, which is too bad for youngsters everywhere.

Sometimes a Circle Isn't a Circle

Who says you can't change the laws of physics, or at least math, with a little creative legislation? Some states simply aren't trying very hard, apparently. A law proposed in Indiana would have established the value of Pi as 3, not 3.1415. The bill was passed in the Indiana House in 1897 but was left pending.

Pending a fifth grade math lecture, perhaps.

PROPOSED
No Fun Outside

Playing outside could become illegal in Volusia County, Florida, or at least in the Persimmon Place subdivision. In 2011, the local homeowners association proposed a ban on kids playing outside unless they have an adult with them. It would ban loud toys, tag and skateboarding to boot.

Parents planned on fighting the "anti-childhood" proposal.

After Wacky Laws: Lawsuits!

It's one thing to pass a crazy law, but it's a whole other thing to sue in a crazy way. Here's a collection of bizarre lawsuits that were filed in the courts.

TRUTH IN ADVERTISING?

Here's the Beer, Where's the Girls?

Everyone has seen the commercials where beautiful women are laughing and having fun while a beer logo flashes prominently across the screen. There's not a beer belly nor a leering drunk in sight, but most of us suspend our disbelief and enjoy the music. *Most* of us.

In 1991 Richard Overton, however, took the ads quite literally. Overton sued Anheuser-Busch in Michigan for false and misleading advertising, claiming to have suffered emotional distress, mental injury and financial loss. The specific ads that Overton felt crossed the line were ads that involved fantasies of beautiful women that came to life to men driving a Bud Light truck. In his lawsuit Overton also notes:

> *…an individual is seen "launching" off a slide and into a somersault. This action alone could result in serious injury by an individual not thoroughly trained in such actions, and most certainly should never be attempted by someone consuming Bud Light. To represent such actions are possible is grossly misleading of the true nature of the product being promoted.*

The lawsuit was dismissed.

I Told You, Close Your Eyes!

Haunted houses pop up all across the country during Halloween, focused on giving every participant a good scare. Cleanthi Peters, though, must have misread the sign at Universal Studios in Florida when she visited the Halloween Horror Nights haunted house. Despite the numerous uses of the word "horror" and "haunted," she was apparently taken aback by the actual scary interior and subsequently sued the park because she suffered extreme fear, mental anguish and emotional distress.

Now that's truth in advertising!

Even more frightening? She was awarded $15,000.

I'm Sexy and I Know It

Penthouse publisher and apparently sensitive guy Bob Guccione sued *Hustler* magazine when his photo appeared in the publication on another model's body in an explicit way, indicating that he'd been unfaithful to his wife. Initially, Guccione was awarded nearly $40 million; however, the case was overturned on appeal. District Court Judge Sweet noted in his opinion that a "considerable amount of time, energy, and money has been expended by counsel by both sides to bring this grudge match to this court."

The judge concluded that since Guccione already had a sullied reputation with respect to fidelity, there was little *Hustler* could do to worsen it.

DISGUSTING OR DISTURBING

Where's the Remote? Hurry!

Ever sit down in front of the television and see something that made you lose your appetite? Austin Aitken had a particularly violent reaction to an episode of *Fear Factor*, where contestants routinely eat disgusting things. In this particular episode, Aitken watched contestants eat rats, and it made him dizzy and caused him to vomit and run into a doorway. He sued NBC for $2.5 million.

The judge ran him out of the doorway. The case was deemed frivolous and thrown out.

Cookie Anxiety

Two teenage girls decided to bake cookies for their neighbors in Durango, Colorado. They wrapped the cookies in plastic, decorated a heart-shaped card and tried to deliver them to Wanita Renea Young at her home. Since it was late, and because no one had ever delivered cookies to her before, Young became alarmed and suffered an anxiety attack so severe that she sued the girls. She was awarded $930 to cover the cost of her emergency room visit but was denied money for her pain and suffering.

BUSINESS CHALLENGES

That Explains the High Prices

In 2007, Karl Kemp had had enough. He owned a high-end antiques store on Madison Avenue in Manhattan and was fed up with four homeless people who congregated in front of his shop.

Since he didn't know their real identities, Kemp sued them under the names John Smith, John Doe, Bob Doe and Jane Doe and asked for damages of $1 million. Needless to say, he wasn't awarded any money, but the homeless people did move along.

Quiet Everybody! Now Pay Up!

Silence, you'd think, is free in the music business. But you'd be very, very wrong. In 2002, the music publishers for the late avant-garde composer John Cage sued musician Mike Batt for plagiarism. Ball had a completely silent "song" on his album.

The publishers claimed the silent song was exactly like Cage's own silent song. Batt settled out of court for what is rumored to have been a six-figure settlement. It seems the sound of silence is more expensive than ever.

COVERING ALL THE BASES

Someone Take Away His Typewriter!

Every vocation has an individual who rises to the top of his or her chosen field and who, through persistence, determination and an abundance of time, achieves what few thought was possible. Such is the case with Jonathan Lee Riches.

Riches, a South Carolina inmate, has filed more than 1000 frivolous lawsuits. He has sued Barry Bonds for $42 million for selling steroids to nuns, Elvis for working with Osama Bin Laden and the planet Pluto for an unspecified civil rights offense, to name but a few. In an impressive act of irony, Riches filed for an injunction against the *Guinness Book of World Records*, which had named him the "most litigious individual in the history of mankind."

The Northern District Court of Georgia has attempted to stem the tide of Riches' litigation, but he has simply moved on to other courts. Riches' original crime was wire fraud.

Take Me to Your Hard Drive

Okay, this is not a law, but a warranty is pretty close. We just couldn't resist including it. Extended warranties can be real cash cows for companies, especially since most consumers don't take the time to read through all the fine print on what is excluded from coverage. The ASUS computer company unveiled its new extended warranty program, and it cited a few of the typical exclusions, such as natural disasters, intentional misuse and improper maintenance. But one exclusion in particular was a little more unusual. The company will not cover damage that comes from "space invasions." Clearly, the company actuaries are taking UFO sightings quite seriously.

The Ultimate Law

In case you had any doubt, a law is created to prevent anyone from committing a particular action. To make it as clear as possible, if there's a law against doing something, don't do it. But in case you need any further explanation, the folks down in Haines, Alaska, have you covered with this next law. In Haines, it is against the law to break any law. It's also against the law to encourage anyone else to break a law.

If, however, a person found guilty of breaking a law wouldn't have been found guilty of the action had "the circumstances been as [the] defendant believed them to be," that person is off the hook! Finally, not only is ignorance bliss, it's also an alibi.

ABOUT THE ILLUSTRATORS

Roger Garcia

Roger Garcia is a self-taught artist with some formal training who specializes in cartooning and illustration. He is an
immigrant from El Salvador, and during the last few years,
his work has been primarily cartoons and editorial illustrations in pen and ink. Recently, he has started painting once
more. Focusing on simplifying the human form, he uses
a bright minimal palette and as few elements as possible.
His work can be seen in newspapers, magazines, promo
material and on www.rogergarcia.ca.

Peter Tyler

Peter is a graduate of the Vancouver Film School's Visual
Art and Design and Classical animation programs. Though
his ultimate passion is in filmmaking, he is also intent on
developing his draftsmanship and storytelling, with the aim
of using those skills in future filmic misadventures.

Patrick Hénaff

Born in France, Patrick Hénaff is mostly self-taught. He is
a versatile artist who has explored a variety of media under
many different influences. He now uses primarily pen and
ink to draw, and then processes the images on computer.
He is particularly interested in the narrative power of
pictures and tries to use them as a way to tell stories.

Pat Bidwell

Pat has always had a passion for drawing and art. Initially self-taught, Pat completed art studies in visual communication in 1986. Over the years, he has worked both locally and internationally as an illustrator/product designer and graphic designer, collecting many awards for excellence along the way. When not at the drawing board, Pat pursues other interests solo and/or with his wife, Lisa.

Djordje Todorovic

Djordje Todorovic is an artist/illustrator living in Toronto, Ontario. He first moved to the city to go to York University to study fine arts. It was there that he got a taste for illustrating while working as the illustrator for his college paper *Mondo Magazine*. He has since worked on various projects and continues to perfect his craft. Aside from his artistic work, Djordje devotes his time volunteering at the Print and Drawing Centre at the Art Gallery of Ontario. When he is not doing that he is out trotting the globe.

Graham Johnson

Graham Johnson is an Edmonton-based illustrator and graphic designer. When he isn't drawing or designing, he…well…he's always drawing or designing! On the off-chance that you catch him not doing one of those things, he's probably cooking, playing tennis or poring over other illustrations.

Craig Howrie

Craig is a self-taught artist. His line art has been used in local businesses' private events as well as a local comic book art anthology. He is also a songwriter working feverishly at a project to see the light of day hopefully within the next decade or so.…

ABOUT THE AUTHORS

Winter Prosapio

Winter D. Prosapio is a writer, novelist, essayist and occasional poet. She co-authored *The Bathroom Book of Texas Trivia* for Blue Bike Books, and her writing has appeared in numerous websites, including Long Story Short and slashfilm.com

Winter is also an expert in media relations and both internal and external communications, with over 25 years experience in Fortune 500 companies, city government and not-for-profit settings. She has opened a theme park, handled all communications for a $2 billion oil-and-gas merger and led a grassroots tort reform movement. Winter and her husband, Adam, reside in Canyon Lake, Texas, with their children Sierra and Mireya, who provide inspiration for Crib Notes, Winter's weekly humor column.

Lisa Wojna

Lisa is the co-author of 16 trivia books, as well as being the sole author of 18 other non-fiction titles. She has worked in the community newspaper industry as a writer and journalist and has traveled all over the world. Although writing and photography have been a central part of her life for as long as she can remember, it's the people behind the stories that are her motivation and give her the most fulfillment.